The Bible On
Revelation

The Bible

on

Revelation

by P. A. ROOSEN

Translated by F. VANDER HEIJDEN

ST. NORBERT ABBEY PRESS
De Pere, Wisconsin
U. S. A.
1966

Nihil obstat: ·

Samuel D. Jadin, O. Praem.
Censor deputatus

Imprimatur:

†Stanislaus V. Bona, D.D.
Bishop of Green Bay
June 1, 1966

The *Nihil obstat* and *Imprimatur* are a declaration that a book or pamphlet is considered free from doctrinal or moral error. It is not implied that those who have granted the *Nihil obstat* and *Imprimatur* agree with the contents, opinions or statements expressed.

Originally published as
De Bijbel over openbaring en overlevering
Roermond and Maaseik, J. J. Romen & Zonen, 1964

Library of Congress catalogue card number: 66 - 22822

Printed in the United States of America
ST. NORBERT ABBEY PRESS
De Pere, Wisconsin

CONTENTS

FOREWORD

Few texts of Holy Scripture describe the whole of Biblical revelation as briefly and as beautifully — even from a literary viewpoint — as does the solemn intonation of the letter to the Hebrews: "In many and various ways God spoke of old to our fathers by the prophets; but in these last days he has spoken to us by a Son, whom he appointed the heir of all things, through whom also he created the world. He reflects the glory of God and bears the very stamp of his nature, upholding the universe by his word of power. When he had made purification for sins, he sat down at the right hand of the Majesty on high" (1:1-3).

These verses could justifiably be used at the beginning of any dissertation on Biblical revelation. They express two main characteristics: encounter and salvation. God addresses man, engaging him in a dialogue in which he reveals himself and draws others into communication with him. This text also clearly stresses the unity and continuity of revelation: it is the same God who speaks in the Old and the New Testament and who brings the former to its consummation in the latter. We say "brings the former to its consummation in the latter"; the author, though pointing to the continuity of the two Testaments, at the same time very markedly expresses the

fact that in Christ revelation has reached its final
form. God, who in the Old Testament spoke only in a
fragmentary way ("in many and various ways") now
in his Son speaks the one word which is all-revealing.

The word he speaks in his Son is so complete and
definitive that with it fullness has arrived — the end
time.

This prologue of the letter to the Hebrews may
guide us in our exposition for still another reason. It
stresses that according to Biblical revelation God
does not usually meet man during his earthly life in
direct and personal revelation; he uses mediators: in
the New Testament his Son, in the Old Testament
the prophets. This shows the importance attached
to these mediators by Scripture. We might feel inclined to accuse the author of Hebrews of bias.
Although it is true that by his word the prophet
was the principal mediator of revelation in the Old
Testament, nevertheless the letter to the Hebrews,
by restricting the number of those who brought
revelation, would seem to have neglected the fact that
there are many bearers of revelation in the Old
Testament, and that revelation by deeds is an essential feature of the Bible narrative. The author may
intentionally have limited himself to summarize the
whole kerygma in a well-balanced phrase. But this
is only an apparent difficulty. When he wishes to
characterize the Son himself as the word of revelation, he does not appeal to prophetic preaching; he
uses ideas taken from the Wisdom books: "a spotless mirror of the working of God, and image of his

goodness" (cf. Wis. 7:25-26). For this reason we can follow his practical way of acting and his implicit view, and speak about the **sage** and the **priest** as the principal mediators of revelation, besides the **prophet.**

There is another feature in Christ being depicted as the ". . . mirror of the working God and image of his goodness" which we should note: God reveals himself by **action.** He makes himself known not only in the words spoken by Christ, but also in the whole of the Son's existence and activity. Certainly, this self-revelation of God through his Son is unique in New Testament revelation. But from this it is only a step to stress manifestation by way of Old Testament facts. The prophets taught this. Because of this we will begin with the fundamental realities of revelation. This will also give some insight into its structure.

Once we see that revelation is an encounter with, or a being addressed by God, we may expect that the explanations about Old Testament revelation will be bound together in the chapter on man's response.

New Testament revelation finds its final unity in Christ; it is possible however to consider different aspects in Christ as he is presented in divine revelation. Since we must restrict ourselves, we will speak of this as it is found in three great complexes: the synoptic gospels, the Pauline letters and the Joannine writings. As regards each of these, we will speak about man's response. We are quite aware that in so doing we still omit important parts of New Testament literature; we also realize that each of the synoptics, though agreeing on many points, has his own theological view. We think however that these three major complexes will give us a sufficient, though perhaps oversimplified, understanding of revelation according to the New Testament. **Tradition** is not dealt with separately because of its close connection with revelation. We have included it in our exposition.

PART I.

THE OLD TESTAMENT

1

THE FUNDAMENTAL
REALITIES OF REVELATION

Semantics of "revelation," and revelation as an event. When one who has no Biblical background reads Holy Scripture to learn its view of revelation, he could easily be disappointed. He might be perplexed to find that the Bible, preeminently the book of revelation, in its Old Testament simply does not know the noun "revelation" as a theological term and that even the corresponding verb "to reveal" frequently has a profane rather than a theological meaning (we find examples of the theological meaning in 1 Sam. 2:27; 3:7, 21; Deut. 29:28; Is. 22:14).

Because of the limited material provided by the Old Testament we might feel inclined to enlarge the vocabulary which we employ to approach the "various ways" (Heb. 1:1) from different sides, to find its full meaning. The resulting inventory is interesting: God "reveals himself" at Bethel (Gen. 35:7), he "appears" to Abraham (Gen. 12:7), he "makes himself known" (Num. 12:6), he "meets" Balaam (Num. 23:3, 4, 16), he "shows his purpose" (Amos 7:1, 4, 7), he "reveals" his secrets (Amos 3:7), he "teaches" man his ways (Is. 2:3) and, especially, he "speaks his word" (Jer. 1:4,

11, 13). By arranging all these different little stones
into a mosaic we should ultimately be able to com-
pose a picture with certain apparent basic aspects.

But this approach does not impress us as the best
way to **introduce** the reader to the Old Testament
view of revelation; nevertheless, we will insert some
of it into our exposition. We must point out a conclusion which follows from what we have said. Our
summary actually indicates a general feature of the
Hebrew mentality; this will be emphasized in our
special inquiry into its concept of revelation. The
Hebrew mentality attaches little importance to the
noun, especially to the abstract noun indicating
something fixed; it focuses rather on the verb: the
Israelite looks chiefly at what goes on, what is
happening, in history.

Hence the most appropriate approach to the Old
Testament view of revelation should be an investiga-
tion of the realities which in the course of Israel's
history commonly were considered God's fundamental
manifestations: the events of the exodus and the
covenant. We would also be correct in beginning
from his communion with the patriarchs. But we
prefer to begin with the events by which the people
of Israel was founded; we wish also to introduce
some important features of Old Testament manifestations which do not stand out so well in the history
of the patriarchs or at least not with the same authority. There is also the fact that this complex of events
was considered by later Israel to be the core of God's

revelation to Israel (cf., as regards the exodus, Jos. 2:10; Judg. 6:13; 2 Sam. 7:23; Hos. 2:16-18; 11:1; Amos 3:1-2; Mich. 6:4; Jer. 2:2; 32:20-22; Ezek. 20:5-10; Ps. 114; Wis. 10:15—12:2; 16:1; 19:21; as to the covenant: Jos. 8:30-35; Hos. 6:7; 8:1; Jer. 11:1-8). Moreover these same events were considered the starting point and exemplar for later (even eschatological) revelations (concerning the exodus: Mich. 7:14-17; Is. 10:20-26 and especially the numerous texts of Deutero-Isaiah beginning with Is. 40; Ezek. 20:32-44; concerning the covenant: Hos. 2:20-24; Jer. 31:31-37; Ezek. 16:60-63; 36:26-28). Last but not least, this complex of events, because of its pre-eminent importance, was accepted as the nucleus around which later experiences and reflections crytallized. Subsequent generations labored intensely to voice these main events, to deepen them and to elaborate them into an Israelitic tradition and historiography. Here we may best expect to reach a somewhat complete and at the same time graphic picture of the fundamental realities of revelation and of the Old Testament view in its very essence.

The exodus as an act of divine revelation. What strikes us at once is the fact that revelation finds its immediate occasion and its context in a factual situation, in this case one of distress and oppression. As an introduction to God's special intervention we find a detailed description of the inhuman treatment and the slavery to which the Hebrews in Egypt are subjected (Ex. 1:8-22).

Then, as a free initiative of God, the whole

complex of revealing acts points to this situation as
an explanation for divine intervention: "The Lord
said (to Moses): I have seen the affliction of my
people who are in Egypt, and have heard their cry
because of their taskmasters . . . I have come down
to deliver them out of the hand of the Egyptians . . .
Come, I will send you to Pharaoh that you may
bring forth my people, the sons of Israel, out of
Egypt" (Ex. 3:7, 8, 10).

The description of the exodus from Egypt forms
a provisory finale for God's activities. Here we may
omit all the intermediate phases amply narrated by
the sacred author and give our whole attention to
the exodus itself, which the Bible pictures as the
crowning event of all that happened previously. Its
core is the passage through the Red Sea, made possible by God's intervention and described in broad
epic style in Ex. 14:15-31.

The many texts which speak or sing about the
passage through the Red Sea and the destruction of
the Egyptian armies, present this intervention as a
unique revelation of God's power and therefore of
Yahweh's innermost being: "I will harden Pharaoh's
heart, and he will pursue them and I will get glory
over Pharaoh and all his host; and the Egyptians
shall know that I am the Lord" (Ex. 14:4).[1]

Here we find the motif which was to govern
Israel's view of revelation: God reveals himself in
a special manner in the **magnalia Dei,** his mighty
deeds in history. The fact that Yahweh engaged

nature in his service and affirmed his dominion in such a way that other gods were brought to nothing has been rightly considered as the very origin of monotheism, one of the chief features of Israelitic revelation. This basic act illuminated the chosen people's religious insight that God's revelation essentially, but not exclusively, manifests itself in historical events; it shows too that the totality of Israel's history, not only its "chief moments," constitutes a revelationary history. This dual viewpoint was, in later times, strengthened by the preaching of the great men of God.

The fact that God's miraculous intervention in the exodus is considered as a starting point may also show that the purpose of these events cannot have been merely restricted to revelation of God's glory (although even in this revelation personal encounter with God is always hidden); he also has decreed to liberate his people. Every act of revealing is at the same time a salutary event. The exodus shows God's mercy and love (cf. Ps. 136:10-15). He reveals himself as the One who immensely transcends all creatures by his might and glory; he is also the One who puts his might at the service of his love. Two points however, deserve our attention: saving activity is provisorily directed only to the welfare of the people of Israel; but when this revelation is developed further the whole of humanity will be involved in this salutary plan. Moreover, God's saving purpose for his people is not limited to mere material salvation from bodily distress and oppression. The exodus

is only the first step on the way which leads mankind into communion with God.

The function of a mediator in revelation. Before
considering this communion with God we must
scrutinize some factors which Scripture closely connects with the exodus; from these the Biblical view
of revelation derives its fuller relevancy.

Scripture has pointed out the obviously natural
and definite character of the circumstances which
made the exodus possible. One of the traditions,
narrated in Ex.14:15-31 and incorporated into the
poetic song of Moses (15:8-9), attributes the Red
Sea's fordability and the destruction of the hostile
army not to God's abolition of the laws of nature
but to a natural event: "The Lord drove the sea
back by a strong **east wind** all night . . . and the sea
returned to its wonted flow when the morning
appeared" (Ex. 14:21b, 27b). But this seemingly
natural event is explained by the inspired author as
extraordinary, a miracle of God who puts nature at
the service of his omnipotence, as a prodigy wrought
on behalf of his people Israel (14:21b Yahweh drove
the sea back . . .; cf. verse 30).

Such an interpretation emphasizes the indispensable
role assigned to the prophet (Moses) in this revelatory event. By themselves the quick drying up of the
straight and the almost-as-sudden return of the
waters might seem to us to be a fortuitous incident.
But these events acquire revelatory value because
of the fact that they were not accomplished in

isolation. They had been announced by Moses who acted in God's name, and in circumstances which made the fulfillment of the promise previously seem utterly improbable. Moses is sent to a powerless, miserable and oppressed people; he is sent by a God whose name is not much more than a mere idea. Moses promises a liberation which neither he nor his people are able to bring about by themselves. At the very moment when everything seems to be lost he once more intervenes to promise, in the name of Yahweh, a liberation which indeed follows: "And Moses said to the people: Fear not, stand firm, and see the salvation of the Lord, which he will work for you today; for the Egyptians whom you see today, you shall never see again. The Lord will fight for you, and you have only to be still" (Ex. 14:13-14).

This connection of promise with fulfillment through God's miraculous activity is rightly considered by some scholars to be a salient feature in the structure of Biblical revelation (cf. Is. 41:21-29; 43:8-12; 44:6-8; 45:21; 48:5). It is found at "special moments" of the history of revelation up to New Testament days (Is. 37:21-37; Lk. 24:44-46). But even on a lower level, where the miraculous factor and its announcement are lacking, Biblical revelation has as a specific feature this mutual link between the historical event as a revelatory act and the interpreting word of God's messenger.

Thus we are directed to the strictly personal element marking every revelation made between God

and his spokesman. The book of Exodus expressly
speaks of the vision of Moses' vocation, where the
prophet is allowed to come in contact with God's
holiness. This theophany or divine apparition is
followed by a dialogue in which God reveals his plan
to save the people and appoints Moses as his deputy
for the execution of this plan. Hence, although we
may say that Biblical revelation is historical, this
narrative of Moses' vocation makes it clear that we
must not understand this history in a too-narrow
sense. God reveals himself, it is true, in an activity
which affects and bears upon a whole people. But
there is also another point in history, no less privileged, where God reveals himself in the person of
the messenger who in this unique experience receives
the insight and duty to proclaim his will, to interpret
his dealings with his people or with mankind as a
revelation, or even enters into them by his personal
cooperation. This indispensable role of mediator of
revelation is a sufficient reason to devote a complete
chapter to it.

The covenant as the aim of revelation. The exodus,
a high point in the events of revelation, does not
constitute their ultimate goal: The covenant has this
position. "He (Yahweh) said: But I will be with you.
And this shall be the sign for you, that I have sent
you: when you have brought forth the people out
of Egypt, you shall serve God upon this mountain."

Recent Biblical science has tended to question the
historical nexus between the exodus and the making
of the covenant, as well as the role attributed in it

to Moses. Some scholars have held the opinion that exodus and covenant were not events that happened to the same group in which Moses was the central figure. According to them, exodus and covenant belong to different tribes or clans, and only at a relatively later time these tribes came into contact with one another. Only then they exchanged their tribal traditions and harmonized the two events. If this view should be accepted in the course of time as more probable, then Biblical revelation would be more strongly accentuated; God's basic revelation would then have been communicated at different places and to different tribes. But it was his plan that these revelations were to grow together. Thus the Biblical presentation of the facts again would be — even in a higher sense — historical. Whether or not the two events originally were historically connected, we still hold that we may follow the description the Bible gives of them.

In the decalogue, or the ten commandments, a very old covenant formula in its essence perhaps dating back to the time of Moses and the Sinaitic covenant, it is especially stressed that the exodus was directed toward the covenant. The stipulations of the latter are closely conjoined with the exodus. They are represented as obligations which follow consequently from the fact that the people was liberated and chosen by God: "I am the Lord your God who brought you out of the land of Egypt, out of the house of bondage. You shall have no other gods besides me. You shall not make yourselves a graven image . . ." (Ex. 20:2-17). A central demand, following as a matter of course from the covenant, is that they shall acknowledge God's exclusive sovereignty over the people of the covenant: "You shall have no other gods besides me." Then follow other commandments or prohibitions, all of which aim at binding the clans to Yahweh or settling the mutual relations between the human partners of the covenant. But all this essentially means that God's dominion is established over a covenanted and united people; it is a dominion which will continuously influence the whole life of the nation, and eventually will extend itself to the whole world. Yahweh here exercises his rights the way the great kings or feudal lords did in the pacts of suzerainty made with their vassals. Though some scholars have said that Yahweh was considered a king — only later in history — perhaps when Israel had come in contact with the Canaanite city states — nevertheless in the Sinaitic covenant God is without doubt considered a ruler and very probably a royal ruler. This conclusion is reached because of the striking parallelism between the form of the Sinaitic covenant and the treaties of suzerainty.

It would however be wrong to conclude from this stressing of covenant rights in the covenant formulas that exodus and covenant themselves simply are interrelated just as are grace and law, gift and claim. We should not see the covenant primarily as something God claimed in exchange for redemption from Egypt. We should emphasize that in the covenant too the aspects of God's mercy or grace prevail; thus it may be seen above all as the continuation and crowning of the exodus.

This twofold aspect of the Sinaitic covenant perhaps might best be illustrated by the way God presents himself in the introductory words to the covenant law: "I am the Lord your God, who brought you out of the land of Egypt, out of the house of bondage." God introduces himself as "Yahweh your God." This expresses two things: He presents himself as dominating and demanding, but also as giving. I am Yahweh your God; I am God over you, the God who lays claim to your exclusive service, because you belong only to me. I am Yahweh your God; I am the God for you, because I reveal myself to you in order to communicate with you. This ambivalence can already be found in the name "Yahweh" itself. As a divine **name** it is probably pre-Mosaic; but Israel understood its full meaning only when God revealed himself in exodus and covenant. Later in Biblical tradition, when trying to explain the name of Yahweh, a double explanation is given, in accord with the more probable etymology which derives "Yahweh" from the verb "to be" (Ex. 3:14). Yahweh is "I am who I am"; this means that Yahweh is a mystery in his very being, inaccessible to man, hidden from his grasp and transcending him immeasurably (cf. Gen. 32:20; Ex. 33:19). But he is also "I am" in the sense of a dynamic and active being, a present being, a being for others. Although God's person is a mystery, totally hidden from man's insight and power, he nevertheless reaches out from himself and offers the mystery of his person for communion in the covenant.

That is why God announces the covenant in this way: "You have seen what I did to the Egyptians, and how I bore you on eagles wings and brought you to myself. Now therefore, if you will obey my voice and keep my covenant, you shall be my own possession among all peoples; for all the earth is mine, and you shall be to me a kingdom of priests and a holy nation" (Ex. 19:4-6). God has lovingly led his people from Egypt to the place of the encounter. The covenant, when lived up to in faith, makes Israel a chosen people, a kingdom of priests, which, representing the other peoples, must dedicate itself continually to the service of Yahweh, its Lord.

Thus it is an encounter, a community of two partners in a covenant, who become allies: "I will take you for my people, and I will be your God" (Ex. 6:7; Lev. 26:12; Jer. 7:23).

As was customary with secular pacts, the Sinaitic covenant finds its expression — we might say its sacramental confirmation — in two different rites. The one, commonly ascribed to the Elohist tradition, has as its main rite the sprinkling of the altar — symbol of God — and the people with the blood of victims. This blood symbolizes the unity of life brought about between Yahweh and his people by the covenant (Ex. 24:3-8). In the second, probably from the Yahwist tradition, Moses, Aaron and the elders of the people — as representing Israel — celebrate a common meal in the presence of God, being allowed to see him (Ex. 24:1-2, 9-11).

In connection with this "seeing God" we must point out a fact highlighted by the series of events related in the book of Exodus; all those events are fundamentally visual in character, or perhaps more accurately, visionary. In some or other way God is said to be "seen." Thus God's glory is shown to the community of his people in the mighty deeds in Egypt and especially in the passage through the Red Sea (Num. 14:22; Ex. 14:4, 13, 17, 18, 31; 15:6, 11-13). But besides this there are at times real theophanies in which God shows himself or his glory, not in his actions but in a more directly visible form; but even in these cases his intimate being remains hidden. Corresponding to such a theophany is vision in man. Thus Moses, when he is called, sees God as an angel of Yahweh, in the shape of a flame of fire. In a similar apparition of a devouring fire Yahweh's glory is shown to all the people on the summit of Mount Sinai (Ex. 24:17; cf. 19:16-20). The events of Exodus undoubtedly owe their fundamental significance for the later history of revelation in Israel in large measure to the preponderance given to this "seeing": a whole community is permitted to be eye-witnesses and beneficiaries of an extraordinary experience of God. This in no way detracts from Moses' uniqueness (Ex. 20:2; 24:16, 18; 34:4-8, 29-35). Some scholars have remarked that in the course of Israel's history of revelation an evolution is noticeable

— already from the time of the patriarchs — in the way God reveals himself; manifestation by way of the word is stressed, while the strict theophany, in which God himself is seen, fades into the background. This is why "seeing" God or his glory more and more becomes the object of eschatological expectation (cf. Is. 35:2; 40:5; 60:1-2), and it was possible to characterize Old Testament revelation as being directed toward "hearing," rather than "seeing." Generally speaking, this view may be called correct, and such an evolution may perhaps be explained by the fact that Israel became increasingly aware of God's transcendence and man's sinfulness (cf. Num. 12:6-8 and Deut. 34:10 with Ex. 33:18-23). But we must not forget that real theophany — God becoming visible — according to the experience of some of the great prophets, such as Isaiah and Ezekiel remains an essential feature of the way God makes himself known, especially when this points to the eschatological future. Therefore the fact that the elders of Israel were allowed to see God when the covenant was made is of very great importance. In this way they learned how intimate would be their communion with Yahweh; they would be allowed to see God himself.

In comparison with this we might be inclined to regard, as less important, other covenant blessings, such as life and peace (Ex. 23:20-31) and even the coming into the promised country; this is avoided if we see all of them as connected with and pointing to higher realities. The covenant between God and

Israel begins a history which develops into a dialogue between God and man. This however is complicated by the fact that Israel is free to refrain from giving a positive response to the God of the covenant and to refuse obedience. In other words, there is a tension within the covenant itself between grace and law. In any event, from the communion of God with man, which is the very essence and goal of the covenant, there springs a history which looks to the future, and has not exhausted all its possibilities in the occupation of the earthly promised land. Just like the God of Abraham, so the God of Moses is not bound by space, nor does he tie his people to a certain place. On the contrary, he is the God of the road (cf. Num. 33-36); he calls his people back from the promised land to the wilderness to speak there to the heart of Israel (Hos. 2:16). His glory is not even bound by the temple (Ezek. 1:3; 3:15; 10:18-22). Yahweh's revelation teaches a religion of ever new roads, leading to one and the same end — the definitive encounter with God.

2

THE PRIEST AND THE LAW

In our first chapter we mentioned the indispensable function of the revelation spokesman. In this chapter and the next two we will look more closely at the principal classes of bearers of revelation, with special attention to their activities. In a pregnant text the prophet Jeremiah enumerated the messengers of his time and their specific characteristics: "Then they said: Come let us make plots against Jeremiah, for the law shall not perish from the priest, nor counsel from the' wise, nor the word from the prophet" (Jer. 18:18).[2]

Priest, prophet and sage: these three classes dominated religious life in Jeremiah's time, but their origin dates further back. We would be wrong if we were to sharply separate them. Even when they were still clearly distinguished, none of them were locked in ivory towers: there were contacts between them, sometimes of opposition and antagonism, sometimes of exchange and borrowing. The pre-exilic prophets, when preaching, based themselves on covenant law and set themselves up as its champions, even though the preservation of the law and its proclamation were the special task of the priests (cf. Hos. 4:1-6). Thus a prophet of priestly extraction like Ezekiel refers to the old temple rituals and makes them serve for his preaching (cf. Ezek. 18:5-9). Scholars have noted the influence of sapiential thinking (as in the description of the messianic ruler in Is. 11:2-5; cf. 28:23-29), in several prophets even though at other times they might fulminate against the sages themselves (Is. 29:14). These sporadic contacts after the exile will develop into an ever increasing rapprochement or even a confluence (cf. in Sir. where wisdom is said to be embodied in the law). But this does not prevent us from considering the three milieus of revelation separately, though occasionally we may be compelled to point to their contacts with the other groups.

We have no intention of sketching an eventual evolution of each of those three classes, inasmuch as there are many uncertainties. Our main purpose is to shed light on the special revelatory activity of each.

The priest and the oracle. First let us consider the priest. Moses himself was probably a priest and because of this he leads the priesthood. We might prove this from texts where he, as a mediator of the covenant, offers the sacrifice and sprinkles the altar and the people with blood (Ex. 24:3-8). Stronger still are the passages where Israel "seeks" Yahweh through the mouth of Moses in order to get oracles: "Now Moses used to take the tent and pitch it outside the camp, far off from the camp; and he called it the tent of meeting. And every one who sought the Lord would go out to the tent of meeting, which was outside the camp . . . When Moses entered the tent, the pillar of cloud would descend and stand at the door of the tent, and the Lord would speak with Moses" (Ex. 33:7, 9; cf. 18:15-19).

The ancient blessing of Moses in Deut. 33 mentions the mantic function of the Levitic priest even before speaking about his giving instructions and his ministry at the altar: "And to Levi he said: Give to Levi thy Thummim, and thy Urim to thy godly one . . . They shall teach Jacob thy ordinances, and Israel thy law; they shall put incense before thee, and whole burnt offering upon thy altar" (33:8, 10). It is normal that the priests — being in this respect Moses' successors — gave oracles in old Israel. Thus soon after the occupation of the promised land we find priests serving in this ministry (Judg. 18:5-6).[3]

Usually these oracles were given by means of "holy lots," called Thummim and Urim. We can see the procedure in such an oracle, in which the answer was given by a simple "yes" or "no" in 1 Sam. 14:41-42: "Then Saul said to the Lord: God of Israel, why hast thou not answered thy servant this day? If this guilt is in me or in Jonathan my son, O Lord God of Israel, give Urim; but if this guilt is in thy people Israel, give Thummim. And Jonathan and Saul were taken, but the people escaped." In Urim and Thummim we undoubtedly meet with a practice and with objects borrowed from the pre-Israelitic culture of Canaan; yet it is touching to see that God accommodated himself to such practices and used them to make his will known. Here we have one of the many cases where Israel's historical and revealed religion took over values from a natural religion. The Israelitic concept of revelation is also characterized by the fact that even when using these instruments of chance they allowed for God's freedom and sovereignty; in certain circumstances he simply refused an answer (1 Sam. 14:37; 28:6).

It would be erroneous to hold that the priest as spokesman of God's revelation had to rely exclusively on these earthly objects, when wanting to give an oracle. He had charismatic gifts for making divine pronouncements. This appears in the oracle obtained by Rebekah in the sanctuary (Gen. 25:22-23). In view of its rhythmical form, this could not have been produced by the above-mentioned practice in which only a "yes" or "no" were possible. Therefore we may understand that the oracular gifts of the priests did not cease when this technical means was discontinued (Ezra 2:63; cf. however a similar proceeding in the early Church, Acts 1:24-26).[4]

Thus we see this oracular charism being practiced when a priest (less probably a cultual prophet; this still is an unsolved problem) answered to the lamentations and supplications of an individual (cf. 1 Sam. 1:17) or of the collected cultual community, and proclaimed in the name of God the oracle he had heard. Thus we see that after a defeat and a collective prayer God answers by giving all at once this oracle, which promises a new national grandeur and restores the frontiers of the former monarchy: "With exaltation I will divide up Shechem and portion out the Vale of Succoth. Gilead is mine; Manasseh is mine; Ephraim is my helmet; Judah is my scepter. Moab is my washbasin; upon Edom I cast my shoe; over Philistia I shout in triumph" (Ps. 60:8-10).[5]

The priest and the torah. The priestly function of being a mediator of revelation comes especially to the fore in the "Torah" already mentioned in the quotation of Jeremiah (18:18). The word "Torah" usually rendered by "law" under the influence of the Greek Septuagint, originally had a considerably broader meaning. It meant instruction, doctrine (concerning cultual, juridical and moral matters) given by divine command (cf. Deut. 33:10 where instead of "thy law" we should read "thy instructions" in accordance with the parallel plural "thy ordinances"). In this broader sense of doctrine or instruction the noun was also used by some prophets to indicate their prophetic word (Is. 8:16; 30:9) or, in the wisdom writings, the instruction of the sages (Prov. 13:14). This however does not prevent that, strictly speaking, the Torah is considered to belong to the priest (Deut. 33:10; Hos. 4:6; Mich. 3:11; Jer. 18:18; Ezek. 7:16; Mal. 2:6-8).

Such an instruction, given by the priest, might concern the difference between what (cultually) is pure or impure, or some practices, such as a ritual fast (Hag. 2:11-13; Zech. 7:1-3 to be connected with 8:18-19). We have another instance, once again cultual, in the so-called "admission torah" or "gate liturgy," of which Ps. 15 is the classic example (cf. also Ps. 24; Is. 33:14-16). When the traveler reached the gate of pilgrims, he asked the priest, as Yah-

weh's representative: "O Lord, who shall sojourn
in thy tent? Who shall dwell on thy holy hill?" As an
answer he received from the priest this instruction:
"He who walks blamelessly, and does what is right,
and speaks truth from his heart; who does not
slander with his tongue, and does no evil to his friend,
nor takes up a reproach against his neighbor; in
whose eyes a reprobate is despised, but who honors
those who fear the Lord; who swears to his own hurt
and does not change; who does not put out his
money at interest, and does not take a bribe against
the innocent. He who does these things shall never
be moved." Thus the instruction ended in a promise
giving verbal expression to the salvation obtained
by being admitted to the temple and to God's
presence.

The decalogue as the nucleus of the Law. It strikes
us that this last torah, though pronounced in a
cultual context, really concerns the totality of moral
life in general; it simply enumerates ten commandments or prohibitions. This immediately reminds us
of the decalogue or the ten commandments, which
are of central importance in the priest's function as
mediator of the law in a stricter sense. The name
"deca-logue" (ten words), considered merely etymolog-
ically, points to an exterior form, to a collection
of any commands or prohibitions in a series of
ten. We find several "decalogues" in the Bible
(Ps. 15:2-5a might be called a decalogue). Usually
however the name is reserved for the decalogue **par
eminence**, found in Ex. 20:2-17 (occurring substan-

tially also in Deut. 5:6-21). This begins with a pro-
nouncement in which God introduces himself before
proclaiming the commandments: "I am the Lord
your God, who brought you out of the land of Egypt,
out of the house of bondage."

These ten words or commandments mentioned in
our first chapter, belong to the true foundation of
Biblical revelation. God, having come to meet man
in the exodus and having chosen him as a partner
in a divine community of life, now manifests his will
as the covenant God. He presents himself as the
Lord who, in the manner of a profane suzerain,
directly addresses and obligates his people authoritatively and in short imperative or prohibitive sen-
tences (the so-called "apodictic" law). He fixes the
conditions to be fulfilled if man is to remain in the
covenant and continue to receive its blessings (Ex.
19:5-6). This covenant law was first proclaimed by
Moses on the occasion of the Sinaitic theophany.
Later it was regularly proclaimed by the priest, as
prescribed in Deut. 31:9-11. This text undoubtedly
reflects a very old custom; there are even scholars
who think that this proclamation was made not
only every seventh year but every other year: "And
Moses wrote this law, and gave it to the priests the
sons of Levi, who carried the Ark of the Covenant
of the Lord, and to all the elders of Israel. And Moses
commanded them: At the end of every seven years,
at the set time of the year of release, at the feast of
the booths, when all Israel comes to appear before
the Lord your God at the place which he will choose,

you shall read this law before all Israel in their
hearing."

Texts such as psalms 50 and 81, which may be
considered to belong to the liturgy of such a proclamation of covenant and law, together with a
minute analysis of the Exodus narrative about the
making of the covenant suggest that the proclamation
of covenant law, together with the tradition of the
mighty deeds of exodus and covenant, took place
within the framework of a cultual theophany, based
on the example of the Sinaitic theophany (cf. Ps.
50:2-3; 81:6, 8). Here we have the same intimate
conjunction of history, law and cult already extant
in Mosaic times; this intermingling is to be lastingly
instinctive of Israelitic revelation, and will determine
the structure of the Pentateuch.

Tradition - evolution - revelation. Before considering the nature of the priestly proclamation of covenant law, we must mention in passing that there were
also other places where God's salutary deeds and
the resulting divine law were proclaimed; this is
especially found in family groups. We find examples
in the historical books (Deut. 6:20-25; Ex. 12:24-26;
13:8, 14-16) and in the Psalms. Ps. 78:3-7 extols the
value of tradition for life: "Things that we have
heard and known, that our father have told us. We
will not hide them from their children, but tell to the
coming generation the glorious deeds of the Lord,
and his might, and the wonders which he has
wrought. He establised a testimony in Jacob, and
appointed a law in Israel which he commanded our

fathers to teach to their children; that the next generation might know them, the children yet unborn, and arise and tell them to their children, so that they should set their hope in God, and not forget the works of God, but keep his commandments" (cf. Ps. 48:71).

We must also indicate that the sanctuary and some religious feasts occupied a privileged place in tradition.

In proclaming the covenant law the priest did not limit his function to an unchanging repetition of the original revelation. The theophany or the religious festivity in which he functioned as the speaker and the representative of the God who continued to manifest his will throughout the history of Israel, entitled the priest to hand down the tradition in a personal way, together with new revelations by which the Old Covenant law was applied to the present circumstances of time and place. We can perhaps see a result of such activity — on the level of a still very restricted covenant law — in the cultual decalogue of Ex. 34:14-26 (though there are scholars who distinguish twelve commandments in it) which again is revealed in a theophany. Both the nature of this theophany and the matter of these commandments — most of them dealing with agricultural feasts — allow us to venture the opinion that the more ethical decalogue of Ex. 20:2-17, appropriate for life in the wilderness, could no longer suffice by itself for the new conditions in the civilized

country of Canaan, and that a new revealing intervention of God was required.

Even though the argumentative value of this latest
example may be disputed, we cannot doubt the
fact that there did exist a living transmission of covenant law, though strictly speaking this does not
imply that this took place only by **oral** tradition or
by the intervention of the priest. As a most striking
instance of this we may consider the **book of the
covenant** in Ex. 20:22. This book, which now is used
in the description of the making of the covenant,
has taken the place of the original book of the covenant, the decalogue; this latter however did not
therefore lose its obligatory character. (Thus Ex.
24:7 in the present literary context concerns the
ample book of the covenant of Ex. 20:22; 23:33, but
in a more primitive phase of the text it applied to
the decalogue of Ex. 20:2-17). This amplified book
of the covenant is rightly considered by some scholars
as the codification of the customs and laws of a
people which (during the period of the Judges) was
settling in agricultural Canaan. What strikes us is
that a great part of this book of the covenant consists of "casuistic" law, which — unlike the apodictic
law (the decalogue) is formulated conditionally as
is a "case" ("If a man . . . then . . ." Cf. Ex. 21:3-11,
18-22, 26-37; 22:1-16). The contents and the form
of this casuistic law largely point to a borrowing from
the non-Israelitic surroundings of Palestine (we say
largely, for Ex. 18:13-27 points out that casuistic law
had come into being already in the desert). Thus

we are confronted with the remarkable phenomenon
that a basically "foreign" law is presented as covenant
law and as the expression of God's revealed will
(Ex. 24:7). Nevertheless we would be wrong in
supposing that the original covenant law (the decalogue) and the later covenant book (Ex. 20:22-23, 35)
are linked only by the fact that both are ascribed
to the revelation of one and the same God of the
covenant. There is a very intimate connection between both these "books of the covenant." In the
latter there are several places where a new apodictic
law occurs (20:24, 26; 22:28-29) immediately endorsed
by the covenant God himself. A part of the decalogue
is now sanctioned by punishment (21:15, 17) or immediately applied to different situations of daily life.

This case of the book of covenant is very en-
lightening for the present purpose because of the
various intertwined elements. Here revelation and
transmission of laws is evidently a process of growth
in which the more primitive decalogue is being
protected, applied and enlarged in such a way that
the will of the covenant God extends his dominion
further and further over the whole life of his people.
Even if according to modern historical views this
later book cannot be ascribed in its totality to
Moses as its author, yet the Bible because of the
nature of this evolutionary process, may rightly
ascribe it to Moses: it breathes the spirit of the
decalogue he proclaimed and it is a later application
of it. This continuity probably played an important
role in ascribing the "new" covenant law to Moses

and at the same time to divine revelation. Moreover, these laws were considered to belong to revelation because of the charismatic function of the various persons who introduced them in Israel. We may think of Joshua (Jos. 8:30-35; 24:25-26) or of the judges or elders whose decisions were considered inspired by God (cf. Ex. 18:19; Deut. 1:17). Although the priests normally did not directly act as judges of civilian or criminal cases, they were consulted as a kind of higher court of .appeal (cf. Deut. 17:8-13). If we consider moreover that the cultual shrines were the obvious places of judgment (cf. Sam. 7:16; 8:2) and that some codifications of law were kept and transmitted under the guard of the sanctuary (cf. 1 Sam. 10:25; Deut. 17:18) we may better understand how the casuistic law (and **a fortiori** the apodictic law) could be considered as inspired by God and inserted into the covenant law.

We might here mention other legal codes, such as the **law of sanctity** (Lev. 17-26) which may very well be connected with the above-mentioned "instructions" about specifically cultual matters; it deals especially with the sacrifices and the rites of priesthood and very definitely delineates the difference between the pure and the impure. Consequently it is a distinctive feature of this law that the observation of the proposed commandments is seen as an imitation, by priests and people, of God's sanctity. This is how this law got its name. This demand for imitation is indicated most clearly by the formula in which God reveals himself as the Holy One: "You

shall be holy; for I the Lord your God am holy"
(19:2). Although the law of sanctity professes to be
a consequence of the covenant (26:42-46) it does
not easily find its place along the line of tradition
we were able to sketch regarding the decalogue;
at best it might be assigned a place at the end of
this tradition.

In order to acquire a proper viewpoint on the
growth and nature of Old Testament law transmission, it is useful to look at Deuteronomy. This is
also professedly a covenant book (28:60). This is
confirmed by its very structure in which most of the
elements of covenant making can still be found.
The covenant law, historically following the book
of the covenant (Ex. 20:22–23:33), is considered to
be the basis of the reformation under king Josiah.
(622), though several elements are much older. Its
purpose is to replace the book of the covenant,
linking up immediately with the decalogue. But
this replacement does not intend a total innovation:
many elements are taken over, although with necessary adaptations, from previous legislation, the result of which is found in the book of the covenant
(cf. Deut. 15:12-18 with Ex. 21:2-6; Deut. 24:10-13
with Ex. 22:24-26). On the other hand several laws
were simply replaced by new laws; for example, the
former custom which acknowledged the legitimacy
of several cultual shrines is now replaced by the
law concerning the one central sanctuary (cf. Deut.
12:5 with Ex. 20:24-26). Typical in this transmission
of laws is the unmistakable evolution in the sense

of a deeper humanity, in imitation of God's own "humanity," "who is not partial and takes no bribe. He executes justice for the fatherless and the widow, and loves the sojourner, giving him food and clothing. Love the sojourner therefore; for you were sojourners in the land of Egypt" (10:17-19). We see the same when comparing Ex. 21:2-6 with Deut. 15:12-18.

We can find a similar progress — no doubt under the influence of the prophetical preaching which together with the priestly tradition determined the spirit of Deuteronomy — in the dominant theme of this book. The binding of man to God (and to his fellowman) which constitutes the core of the decalogue is already seen there as man's grateful answer to God's beneficence; it is freed of the ever threatening risk of becoming merely juridical and legalistic; observance of the law is presented as a grateful and total love of God, in a formula worthy of the New Testament: "Hear, O Israel: the Lord our God, the Lord is one; and you shall love the Lord with all your heart, and with all your soul, and with all your might" (6:4-5; cf. 6:20-25).[6]

We may end this exposition on the importance of Deuteronomy and the law in general by pointing out that here not only the separate "instruction" of the priest (17:19; cf. Jer. 18:18), but also the law as a whole and especially as fixed in writing (Deut. 31:9-11) is called **"this torah"** (17:19; 27:3; 28:61). But this torah, containing divine law above all, still leaves room for history (1:5). This Deuteronomic concept of the torah as a written and relatively ample whole which preaches law and history probably has a predecessor in Hosea (8:12; 4:6 where the knowledge of God also comprises the knowledge of his saving deeds) and will prepare for application of the name "Torah" to the whole of the Pentateuch, where history and law are also joined. This ever increasing extension of the meaning of this word offered several possibilities. Either the whole of the divine revelation was reduced to God's demanding law, absolutized so as to be a fixed unchangeable value: in this direction the torah evolved into rabbinism, which made the law and man himself independent over against God; this established a barrier to God's further intervention in history and ultimately to belief in Christ (cf. 2 Cor. 3:6, 14-15; Rom. 10:3). Or the word continued to be understood in a sense that gives priority to God's activity in history, and therefore could easily be used as a synonym for "revelation" and applied to the whole of Scripture (cf. Ps. 1:2), including its prophetical element (Rom. 3:19; 1 Cor. 14:21). This view allowed Christ to be seen as the fulfillment of the "law" (Rom. 10:4).

3

THE PROPHET AND THE WORD

Early prophecy. As the priest, so also the prophet has his exemplar in Moses. Certainly, because of his unique role in the establishment of Israelitic religion Moses transcends any comparison (cf. Num. 12:6-8; Deut. 34:10). But he has many features in common with the great prophets, such as the experience of his being called, his mission to herald God's will to the people and his activity in history, even though the title of prophet may have been given him only at a relatively late time (cf. Deut. 18:15).

Early in Israel's history we find reference to individual prophetic persons called "seers" who received oracles and were able to see hidden secrets (1 Sam. 9:9; cf. Num. 24:3-4). A chief representative of this class was Samuel. Obeying divine revelation he anointed Saul as leader of the people (1 Sam. 9:1-10, 16), actively intervened in his proclamation as king (11:14-15) and later rejected him by God's order (13:12-14; 5:10-23). Here already we see close unity between the person of the prophet and the history of revelation; Samuel plays an important role in the birth of the kingship so vital for salvation history.

In a sphere different from that of the "seer" the

movement of primitive "prophetism" evolved. Strongly influenced by the Canaanite milieu, it manifested itself chiefly in a wild and contagious ecstasy of whole groups (1 Sam. 10:5-6; 19:20-24), interspersed at times by oracles (cf. the "false prophets" of 1 Kings 22:10-12). From among these prophetic groups in the early period of the kings, Elisha stands out as an eminent figure (2 Kings 2-13).

Against these prophetic communities a few isolated individuals emerge who are also called prophets. Besides Elijah, in whom early prophecy reaches its height (cf. for Elijah as a prophet, 1 Kings 18:36) and who by his forceful action saved the cult of Yahweh from being destroyed in the northern kingdom (1 Kings 17; 2 Kings 1) we must mention Nathan. Because he was a "court prophet" his preaching definitely influenced the history of revelation. His prophecy, promising an everlasting covenant between God and the Davidic dynasty, made him the founder of the royal messiahship: "When he commits iniquity, I will chasten him with the rod of men, with the stripes of the son of men, but I will not take my steadfast love from him, as I took it from Saul, whom I put away from before you. And your house and your kingdom shall be made sure for ever before me; your throne shall be established for ever" (2 Sam. 7:14-16). Though the term "covenant" is not used here, the text expresses its essence; this is confirmed by the last words of David: "Yea, does not my house stand so with God? For he has made with me an everlasting covenant, ordered in all things and secure.

For will he not cause to prosper all my help and my desire?" (2 Sam. 23:5).[7]

Thus besides the Sinaitic covenant, with its tension between election and law, there is now the unconditional Davidic covenant as one of the pillars of the history of revelation, furnishing the basis on which the classic prophets were to build their hopes of salvation.

Classic prophecy and revelation by word. We now focus our attention almost exclusively on these great figures who were active from the eighth century to the exile. We cannot deny a certain continuity between classic prophecy and the preceding earlier prophecy in all its forms (cf. the words of Nathan, above). Some scholars have spoken of a prophetic spirit which inspired the great Yahwist and the Elohist historical traditions (although some join the latter with classic prophecy). It is an indubitable fact that Holy Scripture has retained the preaching of the classic prophets almost exclusively, and they deserve above all others a place in our exposition on the prophet and the word.

In these men, more than in other transmitters of revelation, we see God's free initiative and his sovereignty at work; this is one of the main marks of Old Testament revelation. We see this already in the first of the writing prophets, Amos. The priest of Bethel advised him that for his own good he should leave Israel — the northern kingdom — and make a living by prophesying in Judah. He answered:

"I am no prophet, nor a prophet's son; but I am a
herdsman, and a dresser of sycamore trees, and the
Lord took me from following the flock, and the
Lord said to me: "Go, prophesy to my people Israel"
(Amos 7:14-15).

The distinctive mark of Amos' preaching is that
he does not owe his prophetic word to his own
initiative or to affiliation with a group of prophets;
it derives from a very intimate encounter with God.
He is not a prophet by profession, but only and
solely by divine vocation. There was nothing in his
usual normal activities which destined him to such a
mission. But God entered into his life. He seized
him as he was, engaged him in his service and
sent him. In this encounter he sees something of
God's own nature and we can read in the introduction of his prophecy how terrified he was by this
revelation: "The Lord roars from Zion, and utters
his voice from Jerusalem; the pastures of the shep-
herds mourn, and the top of the Carmel withers"
(1:2; cf. 3:8). Somehow, in a similar way, each prophet
has had his private encounter with God when he
was called. This explains their self-assurance and
confident manner of preaching (cf. Is. 8:11; Jer.
20:7-9) and the details of their vocation.

The message to be carried by the prophet was
often communicated to him by God within the framework of a vision. Amos is an example. Yahweh
shows him five visions, probably at the time he
was called (Amos 7:1-3, 4-6, 7-9; 8:1-3; 9:1-4). Isaiah
(6:1-13), Jeremiah (1:4-19) and Ezekiel (1:1-3, 15)

were also called in visions. But there is a difference with Amos. Although Yahweh is mentioned, the apparitions presented events, actions or material objects. Isaiah and Ezekiel see a magnificent vision of God himself; from their reactions and descriptions it is obvious that the theophany itself is of utmost importance. Nevertheless, these extraordinary apparitions are immediately subservient to the message to be preached. Thus we learn that the vision is not a self-contained revelation: normally, it is directed toward the word.

This word itself has the focal importance. For example, the vocation narrative of Deutero-Isaiah, chapter 40, mentions only the divine voice which calls the prophet to his task and informs him of the message he has to preach: "A voice cries: In the wilderness prepare the way of the Lord, make straight in the desert a highway for our God . . . And the glory of the Lord shall be revealed, and all flesh shall see it together . . . A voice says: Cry! And I said: What shall I cry? All flesh is grass, and all its beauty is like the flower of the field . . . The grass withers, the flower fades, but the word of our God will stand for ever" (Is. 40:3, 5-6, 8).

Thus the word preeminently became the prophetic medium of revelation. Hence it is natural that the divine revelation to the prophets usually is introduced in these terms: "The Lord said to . . ," "The word of the Lord came to . . ."; they themselves legitimize their preaching with "Thus speaks the

Lord." These formulas recur so often as to make it superfluous to give precise references.

This does not mean that every word spoken by the prophet as the word of God can always be traced back to a direct and clearly defined revelation. But either remotely or directly every prophetic word goes back to the experience of divine realities or to the divine mission of the prophet; in them it finds its ultimate source and its unshakable assurance (cf. Jer. 1:9; 20:7-9; 23:16-40). From these texts we see that Jeremiah pointed out the essence of prophetic revelation when, confronting his adversaries, he describes the prophet as mediator of the word (18:18).

The message the prophet thus proclaimed by divine command considers the present status of his people; he again preaches God's demanding will in contrast to the infidelity of Israel.

In his diatribe he accuses the people of the moral and religious disorders which sin against the covenant law: "Hear the word of the Lord, O people of Israel, for the Lord has a controversy with the inhabitants of the land. There is no faithfulness or kindness, and no knowledge of God in the land; there is swearing, lying, killing, stealing, and committing adultery; they break all bounds and murder follows murder" (Hos. 4:1-2; cf. the decalogue). His warning word exhorts them to a renewed fidelity to God and his law: "And the Lord said to me: Proclaim all these words in the cities of Judah, and in the streets of Jerusalem. Hear the words of the covenant and do them" (Jer. 11:6; cf. Zeph. 2:3). Looking back at the old traditions of the past the prophet thus proclaims the will of God for the present moment, reasserting his dominion over his people.

But he also has a message for the future, again striving to reestablish God's kingship. Thus the pre-exilic prophets begin with the sins of the people against the covenant in order to pronounce in threatening words the verdict to be executed on the northern and southern kingdom by the great powers which at that moment determine the course of history. The usual link between guilt and verdict is often shown by combining remonstrance and threat. For Amos, Israel's infidelity to the obligations flowing from their election is the reason for their punishment and downfall: "You only I have known of all the families of the earth; therefore I will punish you for all your iniquities" (Amos 3:2). This divine verdict even goes to the extent of simply abolishing the Sinaitic covenant: "Call his name not my people, for you are not my people and I am not your God" (Hos. 1:9).

But we would err if we considered this verdict the last word of pre-exilic or exilic prophets. By it the chosen people reaches its salvation. The prophetic word about the future is not exclusively menacing; ultimately, it is a promise. The prospect of definitive salvation in future times is presented in various ways. Some foretold that it is to be brought about by a further development of Nathan's prophecy; salvation shall come through the ideal descendant of David who, as a just king or shepherd of the people, will establish justice and holiness, together with messianic peace: he will establish God's kingdom on earth (Is. 9:1-6; 11:1-9; Jer. 23:5-6; 30:8; Ezek. 34:23-31; 37:24-28; Amos 9:11; 13:15; Mich. 4:11; 5:5). Other prophets begin with the fundamental facts of revelation: they announce a new exodus (Ex. 20:32-44; Is. 40:3-5; 41:17-20; 43:16-21 . . .), a new covenant (Hos. 2:10-14; Is. 54:9-10); prescriptions of law will no longer menace the firmness of this covenant, because the law will be written in the very hearts of men by the Spirit of God, and all of them will know God through a personal revelation (Jer. 31:31-34; 32:37-41; Ezek. 11:17-20; 36:26-28).

These texts clearly show that the prophetic preaching, through which God addresses Israel, is also an interpretation of past, present and future history.

This prophetic interpretation of history in a divine context also contains revelation about various aspects of God's nature. Their individual encounter with God and the specific message each of them brought usually emphasizes one or other divine property. Thus Amos chose to accentuate God's justice, Hosea his jealous and merciful love, Isaiah his holiness; Deutero-Isaiah sheds a strong light on his uniqueness (monotheism) and the ensuing universalism of God's economy of salvation.

All these revelations of the nature of God and his activity in history simultaneously contain revelation about man: his nothingness and sinfulness are projected against God's transcendence and moral perfection (cf. Is. 6:5; and the continuously repeated "Son of Man" by which God addresses the prophet Ezekiel; and the clear consciousness of man's sinfulness in Jeremiah, e.g. 13:23).

It may be true that prophetic preaching exaggerates the distance between God and man. But this also sheds a stronger light on God's love; his promise of salvation manifests his decision to bridge this gap. It strikes us that the two prophets who place greatest stress on God's transcendence, also bring him closest to man: Isaiah by giving to the human Messiah the name "God with us" (7:14) and by attributing the names of the divine court officials to the king in the time of salvation (9:5); Ezekiel does the same when he sees the magnificence of the holy God appearing in "the likeness as it were of a human form" (1:26). Each in his own way directs our attention to God's self-revelation in the incarnation.

Classic prophecy and revelation by deeds. The prophet's relationship with history does appear in the word he proclaims about history; it is also manifested in the effective way the prophetical word functions. Because it is the word of God, it shares in his creating or annihilating power, giving movement to events and building up history. When Jeremiah was sent he received power "over nations and over kingdoms, to pluck up and to break down, to destroy and to overthrow, to build and to plant" (Jer. 1:9-10).[8]

Within this framework of effective prophetic words

we must also be able to discern prophetic sign-actions (symbolic actions). A prophet acts in accord with the divine plan; his actions thus become a sign of future events. The course of history which, at a shorter or longer range, is to be begun by God's word is already now embodied in a symbolic action.

We see a most striking instance of such symbolic actions in the life of the prophet Hosea. He is ordered by God to marry a woman who had undergone the initiation rite for wedlock, commonly used in the cult of the northern kingdom, entirely centered on the god Baal. This makes his wife a typical figure of the guilt of Israel, unfaithful to Yahweh because of idolatry — like a lewd woman. Moreover God orders him to have children from this wedlock and to give them symbolic names: "Jezreel," "Not pitied" and "Not my people"; they are living signs of the judgment God will execute against the northern kingdom and the dynasty of Jehu, which had won the throne by the massacre of Jezreel (cf. 2 Kings 9:22; 10:14).[9] Hosea had to experience in his person and in his family all the accusations, admonitions and threats that other prophets could bring to the people in words. God's word was embodied; Hosea's family life became God's revelation for himself and for others, and the profound source of his prophetic preaching (Hos. 1:2-9).

In verbal prophecy the judgment does not constitute the last word; neither is this the case in prophecy by act. After some years the prophet again receives an order: "Go again, love a woman who is beloved of a paramour and is an adulteress; even as the Lord loves the people of Israel, though they turn to other gods . . ." (3:1). He is here invited to clearly manifest, by his love for the unfaithful wife, God's love for Israel; from his own life he was to draw the meaning and the content of his preaching: God's saving love leads us by way of judgment to liberation. The name Jezreel ("God will sow") now symbolizes the fertility of the country; God again has pity on "Not pitied"; and to "Not my people" he says "You are my people" (2:24-25).

These and similar symbolic actions typifying the distinctive features of a particular revelation are often seen in the lives of the prophets (regarding the prophets family life being used in his preaching cf. Is. 8:18; Jer. 16:1-9; Ezek. 24:15-17; cf. other examples in Is. 20:1-6; Jer. 32). These amply demonstrate how the prophet's innermost life is affected by the word; in some cases it is almost extinguished because of God's revelation. That is why Deutero-Isaiah was able to transpose the prophet's life — though colored now with royal aspects — into a prophecy by word; this is the prophetic figure of the Servant of God (Is. 42:1-9; 49:1-6; 50:4-11) who, especially in his zenith as the suffering and reconciling Servant (52:13—53:12), is the most striking type of the suffering and dying Christ.

Prophetic tradition. With this last consideration about the continuity of prophetic revelation we have entered the domain of prophetic tradition.

Some prophets undoubtedly wrote words or stories themselves, or at least dictated them to a confidant; we can surmise this from some narratives where they speak in the first person (cf. Hos. 3:1-5, written in the first person, with Hos. 1:2-9, speaking about the prophet in the third person). Explicit testimonies indicate the same, such as Jer. 36:4 and 36:32 where Jeremiah dictates to Baruch; cf. Is. 8:1; 8:16-18; 30:8; Ezek. 43:11; Hab. 2:2). We can therefore consider these as examples of an early transmission by writing, initiated by the prophet himself.

Other sections were not written directly by the prophet or a secretary, but were preserved for a time in oral tradition, until finally they too were written.

This transmission — oral or written — of the prophetic message was made either individually by an intimate pupil, or by a group of confidants who had gathered around the prophet. Jeremiah had his pupil, Baruch; Isaiah had a group of pupils to whom he confided his revelation (Is. 8:16).

This tradition, expressing in all its various forms prophetic revelation, was kept topical and alive by supplements or interpretative additions of the trans-mitters. Thus at the end of the third chapter of Hosea the expressions "and David their king" and "in the latter days" probably can be considered as a messianic-eschatological view originating in the southern kingdom; it therefore may be attributed to Judean transmitters, who had readily accepted and promulgated Hosea's prophecy: "Afterward the children of Israel shall return and seek the Lord their God, and David their king and they shall come in fear to the Lord and to his goodness in the latter days" (3:5). Such instances of a transmission which actualizes tradition are rather numerous and of considerable length. We cannot deal here with some books, such as Ezekiel, where several chapters clearly have been interpolated with interpretative annotations of the transmitters (cf. the vision of the vocation at the beginning of the book). Among examples easy to obtain we might quote Mich. 1:5c, where a prophecy directed against Samaria is applied to Jerusalem; or Mich. 7:11-13, an oracle promising salvation dating from the exile or after; or a similar oracle of Amos 9:11-15, where the allusion to "the booth of David that is fallen" points to a time later than Amos. Here we find a phenomenon akin to the tradition of laws: tradition becomes "revelation" in a larger sense.

This adaptative and growing tradition of the preaching of the great men of God must be ascribed to circles of their anonymous followers who did not achieve personal prominence. Even the great prophets themselves are not always quite as original and independent in their revelations as one might at first presume. We have already pointed out that in proclaiming God's will they go back to the transmitted covenant law (and to the great traditions of Israelitic salvation history. Deutero-Isaiah (40:55) influenced Third-Isaiah (cf. 58:8b with 52:12b; 62:11 with 40:10; 61:1-3 with 42:1, 7 and 49:8-13). Hosea's proclamation of God's love for Israel under the figure of marital love (Hos. 1-3) was used by Jeremiah (2:2; 3:1, 6-12) and after him by Ezekiel (16 and 23); this thus became the starting point of a long Biblical tradition.

These few instances, taken from among many, sufficiently demonstrate that prophetic "revelation" often uses "tradition" — taking it over, editing it and handing it down in a new way to a new generation.

Apocalyptic writings. In the post-exilic prophetic books we find more and more references to the ancient prophets; this would seem to indicate that, in their opinion, the time of the great classic prophecy had passed (Is. 48:3; Zech. 1:4; 7:7, 12). Zech. 13:2-6 foretells the eventual disappearance of the prophetic office. This prophecy was fulfilled; in the third or second century B.C. conviction is expressed that the prophetic charism has ceased (1 Macc. 4:6, 46; 9:27; 14:41).

From this time on, whatever is accepted as — or claims to be — a prophecy utilizes the device of pseudonymity, the author pretending that his "prophecy" is the work of one of the great personalities of the past, such as Henoch, Moses, Ezra. This happens in the book Daniel (between 167 and 164 B.C.), a writing of special importance for New Testament revelation. It belongs to the apocalyptic movement; this, as the name itself implies (Greek **apokaluptein**= to reveal), is concerned with the "revelation" of heavenly secrets. The apocalyptic has been given the power to see these secrets so that he may comfort those in distress and persecution, by pointing to God's universal predetermining will, and by predicting swift liberation from suffering and persecution. The fact that the good people were then living in a period of severe crisis fostered this apocalyptic trend and made it flourish.

This movement was closely bound to prophecy. Already in the prophetic books we find some texts, in topic or form, showing an apocalyptic character (Is. 24-27; Ezek. 38-39; Zech. 12-14). The apocalyptics identify with prophets, intending to interpret them, as Daniel, for example, refers to Jeremiah's prophecy about the seventy weeks (Dan. 9; cf. Jer. 25:11; 29:10).

But Daniel was also — perhaps even more greatly — influenced by wisdom. As were the prophets, he too is certainly inspired to prophesy the future. But when he receives this revelation he really does not act as a prophet, but rather as a sage: "To thee, O God of my fathers, I give thanks and praise, for thou hast given me wisdom and strength, and hast now made known to me what we asked of thee, for thou hast made known to us the king's matter" (Dan. 2:23).[10]

Unlike the prophetic revelation by word, the apocalyptics — Daniel too — receive their revelations almost exclusively in ornate symbolic or allegoric visions and dreams (Dan. 2; 3:31; 4:34; 5; 7; 8; 10-12), which sometimes are interpreted by an angel (cf. 8:15-26; 9:20-27).

They are further characterized by a sharp distinction — at least an implicit one — between two "ages" or "worlds": "this world" and "the coming world." Evil has so vitiated the present age that salvation and the coming of God's dominion could not lie in any extension of it; they can be brought about only when the "coming age" breaks through into history, conquering the powers of evil and bringing down upon earth its salutary benefices: these are already present in heaven. This evolution of history, with its succession of several world empires until the end time, and with the descent of the reign of the saints (7:18) which also is the reign of God (7:33 (100); 4:31), contains the "secrets" revealed to Daniel (2:18-19, 27-28, 47; 4:6).

The central personality in the founding of this kingdom of God on earth is no longer the traditional royal Messiah of previous prophets; now he is the mysterious figure of the Son of Man who, in keeping with the eschatology of the "coming world," descends from heaven: "I saw in the night visions, and behold, with the clouds of heaven there came one like a son of man, and he came to the Ancient of Days and was presented before him. And to him was given dominion and glory and kingdom, that all peoples, nations and languages should serve him; his dominion is an everlasting dominion, which shall not pass away, and his kingdom one that shall not be destroyed" (7:13-14). This prophecy about the kingdom and the Son of Man brings us, chronologically and mentally, very close to the revelation which will be brought by Jesus of Nazareth.

4

THE SAGE AND THE COUNSEL

In contrast with the priest and the prophet, who had Moses as exemplar of their mission and activity, the sage of Israel finds his archetype in Solomon. This is evident from the fact that many of the wisdom books — Proverbs (1:1; 10:1; 25:1), Ecclesiastes (1:1, 12, 16; 2:7-9), the Song of Songs (1:1; cf. 3:7, 9) and Wisdom (9:7-8, 12) — explicitly or implicitly present themselves as the work of David's immediate successor. They claim this even though only one of them (Prov.) — and this only in part — dates back to him. The first book of Kings also considers Solomon the patron of the sages. Here he is praised as the sage **par excellence,** whose wisdom was great "like the sand on the seashore, . . . (surpassing) the wisdom of all the people of the east, and all the wisdom of Egypt"; this enabled him to utter three thousand proverbs, to write a thousand and five songs and to speak about various trees and animals (1 Kings 4:29 ff.).

This last text allows us to draw an important conclusion: in Solomon's time, within his circle and through his personal endeavor, wisdom as a literary phenomenon was introduced into Israel.

This, naturally, does not mean that true wisdom was previously altogether lacking in Israel. But what existed there was popular wisdom, expressed in popular proverbs. Israel had brought this from the desert; it later increased through contact with the wisdom of the native Canaanite people. We see a typical indictment of such wisdom in 1 Sam. 24:14: "Out of the wicked comes forth wickedness."[11]

There were already in those days individuals considered wise, as was the "wise woman" enlisted by Joab to influence David (2 Sam. 14:1-21; Cf. 2 Sam. 20:15-22).

But there was as yet no class or rank systematically and professionally preoccupied with wisdom. This came only after Solomon's reign. In the Biblical wisdom literature we find a number of proverbs which set up special ideals for people living at the court (cf. Prov. 16:12-15; 20:2; 24:21-22). The same book tells us (25:1) that the officials of Hezekiah, king of Judah, copied a number of Solomon's proverbs. Israel also had contact with foreign (especially Egyptian) wisdom, used for training officials. From this we may conclude that systematic wisdom was originally cultivated in the higher classes and by the officials of the court or perhaps also of the administration throughout the country — among whom there must have been "writers" who wielded a ready pen. Thus, besides the oral tradition, a written tradition of the acquired wisdom was also made possible. Gradually however the circle of the sages was enlarged and democratized, as can be concluded from reference to the wise men whom the writer of the book of Job chose as his model. We might mention too that the sages at the court would not have allowed the treasure of popular wisdom to be lost. Besides coining new synthetic proverbs or adopting non-Israelitic materials (Prov. 22:13; 23:11; 30:1-14; 31:1-9), they also endeavored to gather and arrange already extant popular proverbs.

In mentioning the popular proverb, usually presented in prose, and the more involved synthetic proverb, characterized by poetic form, we have already touched upon the basic genre, the usual form wisdom used to express itself. Especially after the exile we find extensive wisdom poems (cf. Prov. 8:1-36; 9:1-18) which later on will develop into great literary works as Job and the book of Wisdom.

The two types of proverbs may present themselves in two forms. They may make a matter of fact statement: "A slack hand causes poverty, but the hand of the diligent makes rich" (Prov. 10:4). Or they may also take the form of an admonition, indicating how man should act, in view of what has been established before: "Do not speak into the hearing of a fool, for he will despise the wisdom of your words" (Prov. 23:9). This admonition however does not carry the same compelling authority as does a command of law or the word of the prophet. It has the authority of a counsel, the "counsel from the wise" (Jer. 18:18), who tries to persuade because of the reasons he has proferred.

The message of pre-exilic wisdom. When we now ask about the message of wisdom we must distinguish between the theological wisdom of post-exilic times (found in Prov. 1-9), about which we will speak later; and the older, pre-exilic wisdom (in Prov. 10-20). Speaking very generally, we may designate the older wisdom as an empirical insight and an art of living. But "art of living" covers a wide and variegated field for study and comment. We know that the sage speaks about morals and piety; on these subjects he is factual and gives shrewd counsel really worthy of Biblical wisdom. "The fear of the Lord is instruction in wisdom, and humility goes before honor" (Prov. 15:33).

However, it seems peculiar to us that the sage — although in accordance with his origin! — often gives recommendations which are tainted by utilitarian urban morals, pragmatic rules teaching us how to get on in life: "If a great man bids thee come close, keep the distance; he will but bid thee more; do not court a rebuff by wearing him, nor yet withdraw altogether, and be forgotten" (Sir. 13:9-10).

And we are equally surprised when we hear that a good artisan may also be considered a wise man (2 Chron. 2:12-13) or that the encyclopedia of animals and trees, drafted by Solomon, showed his exceptional wisdom (1 Kings 5:9-14; cf. Prov. 30:24-31).

The revelatory character of the message. Having learned this, we might properly ask ourselves how this wisdom — which often strikes us as very earthly, profane and egoistic — could be admitted as a whole into the divinely inspired books, which as such contain God's revelation to man!

First we remark in general that what is true for the message of the other media of revelation also is true here: the Old Testament revelation is in process and evolution. Therefore some "revelations" are true for a certain time or situation, but later are replaced by or sublimized into a higher revelation, the lasting result of which can only be found when regarded from the point of view of Christ, God's Wisdom (1 Cor. 1:30; Col. 2:3).[12]

That there is such an evolution toward a higher level becomes more evident from the growing moral and religious character of Old Testament wisdom. Moral and religious counsels increase in number; wisdom — after the exile — gradually is seen in its relation to the divine wisdom (cf. how in Job 38-39 a very earthly list of questions is put at the service of the glory of God's own wisdom).

This explicit evolution is made possible by the fact that wisdom already had inward support from a religious mentality. Wisdom's proverbs really express only certain regularities of creation, an order planned by God himself and established by him; man, for his part, must measure up to this divine plan.

Meekness and subjection to the divine plan of creation including man, the conviction of human limitation before God, were already basic character-

istics of pre-exilic wisdom (Prov. 21:30); these will
later be the keynote of the post-exilic wisdom books
of Job and Ecclesiasticus, when an all too pedantic
wisdom is in need of criticism because it threatens
to lose sight of its own limitations. Both those books
show — each in its own way — the insufficiency of
human wisdom when confronted with the deepest
meaning of life and put against the mysteries of
suffering, retribution and death: "Then I saw that
wisdom excels folly as light excels darkness. The
wise man has his eyes in his head, but the fool
walks in darkness; and yet I perceived that one
fate comes to all of them. Then I said to myself:
What befalls the fool will befall me also; why
then have I been so very wise? And I said to myself
that this also is vanity" (Eccles. 2:13-15).[13]

Job utters the same truth in a much more positive
way, by stating, in answer to the speeches of Yahweh
(38-41), his conviction that the mystery of creation
and human existence is one of love, only to be
accepted in silence, reverence and self-surrender:
"I know that thou canst do all things, and that no
purpose of thine can be thwarted. Who is this that
hides counsel without knowledge? Therefore I have
uttered what I did not understand, things too wonderful for me, which I did not know . . . I had heard
of thee by the hearing of the ear, but now my eye
sees thee; therefore I despise myself, and repent in
dust and ashes" (Job. 42:2-3, 5-6; cf. Job 28).

Wisdom thus was religiously impregnated in its
earliest presuppositions; it evolved explicitly and con-

tinually into a more religious mentality. But we must admit now that for a long time it kept aloof from Yahweh's historical revelation to Israel. This, it is true, did not prevent some terminological and theological ideas, originating in the Israelitic salvation history, from having exercised their influence at a rather early date. Nevertheless, explicit reference to God's revelation to Israel is never found. God — who in Proverbs still is called Yahweh, but in Job very seldom and not at all in Ecclesiastes — is never presented as the God of Israel or the God of the forefathers, and only occasionally as Creator (Prov. 14:31; 17:5).

Here we meet with a remarkable phenomenon, especially since we have emphasized revelation through history as essentially distinctive of Old Testament revelation; it is above all concerned with the relationship of Yahweh to Israel and with the dominion of the God of the covenant over his people. We are still more amazed by this phenomenon when we recall that pre-exilic wisdom, though reverencing God and his ordinances, ultimately is not directed toward him, but really toward man; it strives to teach the art of dominating the created world and life in general, theoretically and practically, by arranging everything in a wise manner. This is the primary role of the proverb: it fixes and puts into words a seemingly incalculable and ever variable reality, and in this way brings it under man's dominion. Obviously, the earthly questionnaire of Job. which catalogues natural phenomena, animals and

plants, serves the same purpose (cf. 1 Kings 5:9-14;
Prov. 30:24-31).

There is nothing wrong with this worldly wisdom;
man, independently of any historical revelation but
deferring to the ordinances imposed by God, inter-
feres with creation, arranges it and dominates it.
This wisdom is also acknowledged by the non-
sapiential writings of the Bible; they describe it as
willed by God. When in Yahwistic primordial history
God allows Adam to name all the animals, he
acknowledges man's right to dominate creation by
designating and arranging things (Gen. 2:19-23).
Less ornately, but more extensively, we learn the
same from the priestly tradition, where the Creator
blesses the first human couple and assigns to them,
as the image of God, dominion over the creation
(Gen. 1:28).

Now we understand more clearly why the Bible
considers wisdom in its various forms to be inspired
by God. God himself has revealed this! Faith traditions play an important role in the doctrine of
wisdom. Experience is another major element. "Both
the gray-haired and the aged are among us, older
than your father . . . I will show you, hear me; and
what I have seen I will declare (what wise men
have told, and their fathers have not hidden" (Job
15:10, 17-18).[14] There is no doubt whatsoever that
the Bible ascribes both tradition and experience
ultimately to divine inspiration.

Solomon's wisdom, used in the service of his encyclopedic knowledge, in the formulation of his proverbs as well as in his governmental policies, is given him by God (cf. 1 Kings 3:6-14; 5:9-14; 10:6-7, 23-24; regarding David, 2 Sam. 14:17, 20). Looking at another extreme of "wisdom," this time in an agricultural sense, we find that this art too is ascribed to the inspiration of God's wisdom (Is. 28:23-26, 29).

We conclude that, in the eyes of Israel and its sages, human wisdom, surpassing any mere technical skills must necessarily be ascribed to God's inspiration. We find this conviction confirmed in different texts of wisdom literature, among others in this proverb: "The spirit of man is the lamp of the Lord, searching all his innermost parts" (Prov. 20:27). Or: "For the Lord gives wisdom; from his mouth comes knowledge and understanding" (Prov. 2:6; cf. Sir. 39:6).

This conviction existed already in ancient times; in 2 Sam. 16:23 the counsel of Achitophel is compared to a word or an oracle obtained from God. An inspirational character is attributed to wise counsel and this bears a certain likeness to the prophetic word. The sages were sincerely convinced that their wisdom proverbs in certain cases bore this character, akin to prophetic inspiration. This is evident from the speech of Eliphaz, when he gives a detailed description of a "prophetic" experience of revelation from his own life!

The personification of divine wisdom. Hitherto we have dealt with the early wisdom, although we occasionally touched on matters dating from after the exile. Now we will speak specifically about post-exilic wisdom.

A first characteristic of this wisdom, here understood as the object of systematic reflection, is that it is increasingly personified and identified with God. Job 28 still considered wisdom as an object to be discovered. Prov. 1-7 presented it explicitly as a person (1:20-23; 8-9), begotten by God before all creatures (8:22-26), and present at creation: "When he established the heavens, I was there, when he drew a circle on the face of the deep . . . then I was beside him, like a master workman (favored child), and I was daily his delight, rejoicing in his inhabited world and delighting in the sons of men" (Prov. 8:27-31).

It is quite possible that the original Hebrew text saw this presence of wisdom as that of a favored child playing in the workshop of his father. In this case, no active participation in creation would be intended (the same Hebrew word is translated by some as "child," by others as "foreman"). Later tradition, of both Jewish scribes and Greek Septuagint, understood this presence of personified wisdom as an active participation, such as befits a foreman. Later, in the last wisdom writings, the book of Wisdom unmistakably mentions an active role in the creation: "I learned what is secret and what is manifest, for wisdom, the fashioner of all things, taught me" (7:21; cf. 8:4-6; 9:9).

Although it is impossible to determine in such texts where poetic personification ceases and wisdom is given a true personality, it should be noted that in the course of the revelation personal traits, heavenly characteristics and intimacy with God are more and more emphasized. According to Sir. 24:3 wisdom came forth from the mouth of the Most High; according to Wis. 9:4 she takes her seat at God's very throne: "Give me the wisdom that sits by thy throne, and do not reject me from among thy servants" (cf. 7:25-26; 8:3).

Wisdom as a mediator of revelation. Considering her presence at the creation — as a model or as a workmaster — and her insight into the secrets of creation (cf. Wis. 7:17-21; 8:8) we may easily understand how wisdom can act as a mediator of revelation for all of mankind. God's knowledge manifests itself in creation and on this account is accessible to all men: "To you, O men, I call, and my cry is to the sons of men . . . rejoicing in his inhabited world and delighting in the sons of men" (Prov. 8:4, 31). The view — already implicitly present in early wisdom — that there is a general revelation outside Israel is asserted and taught explicitly here.

Sirach underlines the privileged position of Israel by placing after this universal revelation of wisdom to all nations a special revelation made to Israel, in which wisdom acquires its purest embodiment in law: ". . . in every people and nation I have gotten a possession. Among all these I sought a resting

place; I sought in whose territory I might lodge.
Then the Creator of all things gave me a command-
ment, and the one who created me assigned a place
for my tent . . . All this is the book of the covenant
of the most high God, the law which Moses commanded us as an inheritance for the congregations
of Jacob" (Sir. 24:6b-8; 23; cf. Bar. 3:9; 4:4).

Wisdom as a mediator of revelation is presented,
under the influence of prophetic literature, as a
prophet. She speaks to people on the streets and
squares (Prov. 1:20-21; 8:2-3) as did the messengers
of God (cf. Jer. 5:1; 7:2), and she asks them to make
the decision between life or death (3:21-22; 4:13, 22;
8:35-36).

The message of divine wisdom. When asked for
the message of this wisdom we surely must include
the early proverbs; these, because of their number,
have an important place in two books (Prov. and
Sir.) where personified wisdom holds the center.
Nor can we exclude the considerations of Sir. (44:1;
49:16) and Wis. (10:1; 19:22) about the Israelitic
history of salvation.

There has been an evolution in the doctrine of
wisdom; now it deals with higher realities. In this
connection the book of Wisdom uses the terms
"mystery" and "truth" (2:22; 3:9; 6:22). The mysteries
concern God's plan for man's salvation and the
reward reserved for the just after this life. What
the Wisdom of Solomon teaches on this subject,
probably using Greek thoughts about the immor-

tality of the soul, constitutes a definitive progress
in the doctrine of retribution: "But let our might
be our law of right, for what is weak proves itself
useless . . . There going from us was thought to
be their destruction; but they are at peace. For
though in the sight of men they were punished, their
hope is full of immortality. Having been disciplined
a little, they will receive great good, because God
tested them and found them worthy of himself . . .
They will govern nations and rule over peoples, and
the Lord will reign over them for ever. Thou who
trust in him will understand truth" (2:11; 3:3, supplemented by 3:4-9).[15]

But in wisdom's revelation of mysteries more
attention is given to her own nature and her relationship with God (Wis. 6:22; cf. Sir. 1:6; 4:18; 6:22).
Indeed we might even say that in her essence
she is a revelation of God (Wis. 7:26). This is why
the heights of wisdom literature are reached in the
passages where wisdom reveals her own being in
self-description (Prov. 8; Sir. 24) or where the author
himself describes the essence of Wisdom (Wis. 6:22;
8:16): "For she is a breath of the power of God,
and a pure emanation of the glory of the Almighty;
therefore nothing defiled gains entrance into her.
For she is a reflection of eternal light, a spotless
mirror of the working of God, and an image of his
goodness. Though she is but one, she can do all
things, and while remaining in herself, she renews
all things; in every generation she passes into holy
souls and makes them friends of God, and prophets;

for God loves nothing so much as the man who lives
with wisdom" (Wis. 7:25-28).

It occurs to us that wisdom, originally so objec-
tively earthly and without reference to the historical
revelation in Israel, here has reached real heights;
it shows God's self-revelation, not only as regards
man, but as he is in himself. This is so developed and
so elevated that it could be literally accepted by
Paul, John and the author of the letter to the
Hebrews to express their deepest experiences or
insights into the definitive self-revelation of God in
Christ.

5

THE RESPONSE OF MAN

Revelation is God's coming out from himself toward man; he addresses his creature. Since it is an encounter of two persons it does not attain its essential aim if the second partner fails, if man refuses to go to meet God. Here we will sketch this response of man to God.

Faith and confession of faith. Man's first basic attitude is described when God identifies patriarchal history with Israel and promises Abraham and the barren Sarah numerous offspring. In answer to this paradoxical promise — humanly speaking it could not be fulfilled — Abraham did the only thing possible: "He believed" (Gen. 15:4-6). He disregarded human impotence and relied solely on the omnipotence of God, in whom he placed his belief and confidence.

We find this faith man's normal response to divine revelation, at all decisive moments of salvation history whenever God puts his power at the service of his people or of selected individuals. The story of the miraculous passage through the Red Sea is concluded with the statement: "And Israel saw the great work

which the Lord did against the Egyptians, and the
people feared the Lord; and they believed in the
Lord and in his servant Moses" (Ex. 14:31).[16]

But faith does not remain enclosed in the heart;
Gen. 15:6 already states that it is expressed in
external confession. In ancient Israel the mighty
deeds of God became the object of a confession of
faith as expressed in the formula: "The Lord who
brought Israel up out of Egypt" (cf. Jos. 24:17). The
ampler formulations such as we find in the so-called
"little Creed" recited by the Israelites on the feast
of the firstlings are very old: "A wandering Aramean
was my father; and he went down into Egypt and
sojourned there, few in number; and there he became
a nation, great, mighty and populous. And the
Egyptians treated us harshly, and afflicted us, and
laid upon us hard bondage. Then we cried to the
Lord the God of our fathers, and the Lord heard
our voice, and saw our affliction, our toil, and our
oppression; and the Lord brought us out of Egypt
with a mighty hand and an outstretched arm, with
great terror, with signs and wonders; and he brought
us into this place and gave us this land, a land
flowing with milk and honey" (Deut. 26:5-9).

Some scholars go so far as to say that this creed
is of such importance that it should be accepted as
the core of the great traditions, the Yahwist and the
Elohist; they are the basis of the Pentateuch. These
historical narratives therefore not only exhibit God's
revelation but also show the result of man's response.
More correctly however, other scholars seek the orig-

inal nucleus of the great tradition in the covenant formula, contained in the decalogue conjoining covenant and covenant law with the exodus.

Praising God. Although we grope in darkness concerning the above-mentioned traditions or writings, we can be positive as regards another section of Biblical literature, the Psalms. As a whole, they may be considered man's answer to the essential revelations of God. This is why almost all phases of revelation have found an echo and are represented in their poetry. In them we find the law of the priest (Ps. 19:8-15; 119), the oracle of the prophet (2; 75; 96; 98; 110), prophetic historiography (106), the doctrine of wisdom (1; 37; 49; 73; 128). They best of all teach us what revelation is, because they express the feelings and attitudes it encourages. In meditation and prayer, in cult and confession of sin the group or the individual come into God's presence and engage themselves in that revelation.

Here we will point only briefly to a special form of psalm-prayer, the psalm of praise; this can be considered the most perfect human response. The Hebrew text uses it as the title to the entire book. Whenever God reveals himself to man through word or deed or theophany, man should realistically and exclusively submit himself adoringly in praise of God's majesty. Faith becomes praise: "He rebuked the Red Sea, and it became dry; and he led them through the deep as through a desert. So he saved them from the hand of the foe, and delivered them from the power of the enemy. And the waters covered their adversaries; not one of them was left. And they believed his words; they sang his praise" (Ps. 106:9-12). This last verse alludes to the ancient song of Moses, Miriam and all the chosen people glorifying God's power in choir after passing the Red Sea: "Sing to the Lord, for he has triumphed gloriously; the horse and his rider he has thrown into the sea" (Ex. 15:21).

Henceforth this praise will never die down in Israel's history. It will be the answer to the revelation of God's power in salvation (Ps. 136, "the great Hallel") and to judgment (78), and to the manifestation of his glory and wisdom in nature (19a; 29; 104). This praise pervades all layers of literature, and is crowned in the hymns of Mary and Zechariah (Lk. 1:46-55; 1:68-79), expressed in the revelation of eschatological salvation.

Obedience, love and fear of the Lord. Besides faith, confession of faith and praise we must also mention obedience. This, like faith, is simply a specification of the general attitude of "hearing" in which Old Testament revelation normally is received or accepted. God's beneficence cannot be separated from the covenant commandments which manifest his will. God's chosen ones must obey this will.

Obedience, according to the apostle Paul, is the distinguishing mark of a man really governed by faith in the promise. God summoned Abraham to leave his country and his home, to offer his son as a pleasing sacrifice and to walk in God's presence and be blameless (Gen. 12:1; 22:2; 17:1).

This is even more true for the people of Israel, who live under the economy of the law. When, by God's order, Moses demanded obedience and observance of the covenant commandments, the entire people answered together: "All that the Lord has spoken we will do" (Ex. 19:8; 24:7; cf. Jos. 24:21-24; 2 Kings 23:3). Older texts (Ex. 20:6) do not see this obedience to the commandments as slavish subjection, but as an expression of gratitude and love; this attitude is later developed in depth by Deuteronomy (Deut. 11:13, 22) under the influence of the prophetic movement.

Obedience also originates in another — perhaps more spontaneous — human response to God's revelation: a religious fear of God. According to the narrative of Ex. 19:16-20 the making of the covenant and the proclaiming of the law are accompanied by thunderclaps, lightning, clouds, smoke and fire. Such phenomena are signs of God's majesty, which in turn is the outward manifestation of his sanctity. God's sanctity is a devouring fire. It cannot enter into communion with sin; it brings death to sinful man. A normal response of a creature to a theophany is the fear of Yahweh: "All the people trembled" (Ex. 19:16; 20:18). God does this purposely: he manifests his glory in order that they may fear him and thus avoid sin (Ex. 20:20).

Finally, wisdom too, though it cannot act with

the same compelling authority, demands subjection
and obedience: "And now, my sons, listen to me . . .
Hear instruction and be wise, and do not neglect
it" (Prov. 8:32a, 33).

Conversion. The course of history increasingly
confirms the experiential conviction that opposing
attitudes of unbelief, self-exaltation and disobedience
not only belong to the realm of possibilities but are
all too often painful realities. A prophet appears,
threatening judgment and downfall. His prophetic
word, as does every word of God, demands belief.
Moreover, because the situation has been changed
by apostasy and unfaithfulness, conversion or turning
back is demanded; the sinner must mentally and
operatively turn from evil and turn himself entirely
to God. Thus Amos, after enumerating various
divine judgments, consistently concludes by way of
refrain: "Yet you did not return to me, says the Lord"
(Amos 4:6-11).

The invitation to return is so very central in the
preaching of the prophets as to make it superfluous
and impossible to quote all texts on this topic (some
of the more obvious: Hos. 6:1-6; Is. 1:15-20; Jer.
3:12-14; 3:21; 4:4; Ezek. 18:1-32). We can surmise
how important this topic is in prophetic preaching
from the fact that it was embodied in the figure of
one of Isaiah's sons: "A remnant shall return" (Is.
7:3; 10:21), who thus became an everlasting message.

The reaction on man's existence. In concluding
our consideration of man's response to divine revela-

tion we must note that it is important to understand that the "yes" or the "no" penetrates to the very depths of human existence. This makes it understandable why the texts quoted seldom by-pass the effect their attitudes had on this existence.

When the well-known text of Genesis concerning Abraham's faith adds: ". . . and he (Yahweh) reckoned it (the faith) to him as righteousness" (Gen. 15:6) it shows that by his faith Abraham acted in accord with the communion existing between God and him; in this way he remained faithful to God and could continue living in communion with him.

Isaiah shows us the reverse. He concludes God's promise that the hostile neighboring states of Aram and Ephraim shall be powerless against Jerusalem by threatening: "If you will not believe, surely you shall not be established" (Is. 7:9). On the contrary, he who believingly relies on the cornerstone God has laid in Zion shall not totter (Is. 28:16; cf. also the important text of Hab. 2:4).

Strange though it may seem, the praise of God is in a special way akin with life and death. More than one psalm emphatically establishes that in death there is no longer possibility of praising God: "Turn, Lord, save my life; deliver me for the sake of thy steadfast love. For in death there is no remembrance of thee; in Sheol who can give thee praise" (Ps. 6:5-6).[17] From this we may gather that praise of God is the most proper kind of human existence. Praising and not praising are opposed as are life and death. We might say with little exaggeration that who praises God, lives; who does not praise God is under the spell of death.

The Bible establishes a parallel relationship between obedience and life on one hand, disobedience and death on the other. He who obeys may count on salvation and God's blessings; but he who is unfaithful becomes the object of God's curse (Ex. 23:20-33; Deut. 28; Lev. 26; Ps. 15:5). Obedience to God's will, expressed in law, merits life; disobedience brings death. "You shall therefore keep my statutes and my ordinances, by doing which a man shall live: I am the Lord" (Lev. 18:5).

The same is true of wisdom. In its primitive phase, when it sought to be an art of living, and a control of living, it brought life to all who followed the counsel of the sages. This applies in an even deeper sense to personified wisdom; this gives man a choice between life or death, just as the prophets did: "Happy are those who keep my ways. Happy is the man who listens to me, watching daily at my gates, waiting beside my doors. For he who finds me finds life and obtains favor from the Lord; but he who misses me injures himself; all who hate me love death" (Prov. 8:32b, 34-36).

The book of that name sees wisdom as completely directed to salvation: "And thus the paths of those on earth were set right, and men were taught what pleases thee, and were saved by wisdom" (Wis. 9:18). But this book, which embodies evolution in the doctrine of retribution, resolutely places life, offered by wisdom on an unearthly level. By knowing personified wisdom man acquires intimacy with God and participates in his immortality (6:8-19; 8:13, 17; cf. 2:21; 3:9).

As we already said, the judgment of death, pronounced by the prophet against the sinner, does not constitute God's last word: by censuring Israel's disobedience he wants to bring it back to a new life. The judgment aims at conversion which leads to life. Amos does not simply threaten Israel with certain downfall when it has refused to return to God (Amos 4:6-12). He insistently and urgently invites: "Seek the Lord and live, lest he break out like fire in the house of Joseph, and it devour, with none to quench it" (Amos 5:6).

Seldom has the alternative of conversion and life or obduracy and death been described as vividly as in Ezekiel, the prophet who was a witness of the destruction and exile of his people. He did not consider this choice an intellectual and calculated one; it is wholly dominated by the love of God, who insists on conversion and life: "Therefore I will judge you, O house of Israel, every one according to his ways, says the Lord God. Repent and turn from all your transgressions which you have committed against me, and get yourselves a new heart and a new spirit! Why will you die, O house of

Israel? For I have no pleasure in the death of any one, says the Lord God; so turn and live!" (Ezek. 18:30-32).

How earnestly God was concerned with the life of the sinner, with the "Yes" of man, was to be fully manifested only when he sent his own Son.

PART II

THE NEW TESTAMENT

1

THE SYNOPTIC GOSPELS

In all the synoptic gospels (Matthew, Mark and Luke) we find the certain conviction that Biblical revelation reached a definitive stage within their own era. This is shown in a literary way by the solemn manner in which the evangelist Luke announces the beginning of this stage and relates it to the religious history of the Jewish people and with the history of the world (3:1-2). Although the gospels show the conviction that something real is now taking place, they also affirm continuity between the old and the new revelation: revelation in Israel and revelation in Christ.

Christ the prophet. Jesus of Nazareth takes his place among the great men of God who in the Old Testament were considered the privileged distributors of revelation, the prophets. He acknowledged his prophetic office when he said of himself with regard to his coming death: "It cannot be that a prophet should perish away from Jerusalem" (Lk. 13:33). And when the humble son of the carpenter, filled by the Spirit, returned to his own village to let his fellow citizens share in the gifts of the Spirit, he described his mission in the same words used by an Old Testament prophet (Is. 61:1-2) to show his own, and at the same time the Christ's, mission: "The Spirit of the Lord is upon me, because he has anointed me to preach good news to the poor. He has sent me to proclaim release to the captives and recovering of sight to the blind, to set at liberty those who are oppressed, to proclaim the acceptable year of the Lord" (Lk. 4:18-19).

Like the Old Testament prophets, Jesus announced God's plan by his word: either in promises of salvation (Mt. 5:3-13=Lk. 6:20-23; Mt. 13:16-17=Lk. 10:23-24; Mk. 10:29-30), or in threatening sermons (Lk. 6:24-26; Mt. 11:21-23=Lk. 10:13-15; Mt. 23: 13-36=Lk. 11:42-52). Like the men of God of the Old Testament, he gave expression to his words and at the same time an inchoative realization by using actions as prophetic signs. Thus he depicted the threat made in the parable of the barren fig tree (Lk. 13:6-9) in a symbolic act by cursing it — a figure of an obdurate and unbelieving Israel (Mt. 21:18-19= Mk. 11:12-14, 19-21).

We can readily understand why, after Jesus' death, the disciples of Emmaus could praise him as "a prophet mighty in deed and word" (Lk. 24:19).

But Jesus, even as a prophet, cannot simply be aligned in the series of prophets. Because the revelation he brings is conclusive, he must be considered **the** prophet, the eschatological prophet whom Moses, according to the Jewish interpretation of Deut. 18:19 had promised for the end time to preach to the people of God in a manner never to be equalled.

What the crowd proclaimed at Jesus' entrance in Jerusalem: "This is **the** prophet" (Mt. 21:11; cf. Jn. 6:14; 7:40; Acts 3:22-23; 7:37) had been revealed by the Father himself at the extraordinary glorification of Christ in the transfiguration. Then the Father in the presence of the privileged disciples placed Jesus over against Moses and proclaimed that in him — the Son, the Beloved — the fulfillment of the Mosaic promise had come: "This is my Son, the Beloved; listen to him" (Mt. 17:5=Mk. 9:5=Lk. 9:35).

The proclamation of the new law. In proclaiming God's will in the sermon on the Mount Jesus is the counterpart of Moses: "You have heard that it was said to the men of old: You shall not kill; and whoever kills shall be liable to judgment. But I say to you that every one who is angry with his brother shall be liable to judgment . . . You have heard that it was said: You shall not commit adultery. But I say to you that every one who looks at a woman lustfully has already committed adultery with her in his heart . . ." (Mt. 5:21-48). Christ fulfills the Old Testament prophetic word and mission by his own prophetic message and activity. He acts as the fulfiller of that other ancient revelation, the law: "Think not that I have come to abolish the law and the prophets; I have come not to abolish them but to fulfill them" (Mt. 5:7). Strictly speaking Jesus brings the fulfillment of the Mosaic law by making a practical distinction between its rules for cult and rites and its moral commandments (Mk. 7:14-23=Mt. 15:10-20; cf. Mk. 2:23-28=Mt. 12:1-8=Lk. 6:1-5; Mt.

23:16-26). In the latter he discovers the permanent core of the law. He reduces it to the original order of creation (cf. Mt. 5:22, 28, 33-47) and impregnates it with evangelical love of God and fellowman (Mt. 22:34-40=Mk. 12:28-34=Lk. 10:25-28). Creation itself (Mt. 5:31-32; 19:18) he deepens, interiorizes and radicalizes. The new law consists in imitating God's own perfection (Mt. 5:48).

How Christ in the sermon on the mountain criticizes, radicalizes or changes the Old Testament law, without any appeal to a Bible text, is evident from his his words "But I say to you"; this is a striking parallel to the formula of divine self-manifestation with which the decalogue begins (Ex. 20:2; Deut. 3:6), or which runs as a theme throughout the laws of the sanctity code (Lev. 18:2, 4, 5, 6). Here already we find a self-revelation of Christ; by it he places himself beside God or even in his place.

The proclamation of the kingship of God by word and deed. Eschatological fulfillment of the **torah** is not an isolated item in Christ's revelation; on the contrary, it has a close relationship with the central theme of his preaching, as he himself declares: "Whoever then relaxes one of the least of these commandments and teaches men so, shall be called least in **the kingdom of heaven;** but he who does them and teaches them shall be called great in the **kingdom of heaven.** For I tell you, unless your righteousness exceeds that of the scribes and pharisees, you will never enter the **kingdom of heaven"** (Mt. 5:19-20; cf. 6:33).

God's dominion was included in the Sinaitic covenant as a demand and as a promise. Because of the
failure of this kingdom of God during the period of
the kings, the prophets promised it as a future
reality. In the midst of the political and religious
dislocation, seemingly promising no hope for the
future, the apocalyptics were able to behold it as
already existing in heaven and foretold its appearance in "this world" in the near future. Now Jesus
appears with the joyful message "The kingdom of
heaven is at hand" (Mt. 4:17=Mk. 1:14-15). The
synoptic gospels link this preaching with the prophetic message of the Old Testament. Thus in Lk.
4:16-21, where Jesus, as fulfillment of the prophetic
figure from Is. 61 preaches the **good news** to the
poor and the destitute together with the adjoining
text of Lk. 4:43 about his being sent to preach the
good news of the **kingdom of God,** points to the topic
clearly expressed in Is. 52:7: "How beautiful upon
the mountains are the feet of him who brings **good
tidings,** who publishes peace, who brings good tidings
of good, who publishes salvation, who says to Zion:
Your God reigns" (cf. 40:1-5, 9, 11).

Other synoptic texts, to be considered later, evidently go back to the apocalypse of Daniel.

Jesus was able to announce the approach of the
kingdom of God with extraordinary authority because
in himself he bore the power to bring it about. Just
as later, with reference to Jerusalem, he was to
embody the judicial aspect of God's kingdom in the
miracle of the cursed and withered fig tree, so now

he embodied the salutary aspect of this kingdom in cures and exorcisms. We have established that a normal trait of Old Testament revelation is its promulgation by deeds: the word God speaks is filled with the power of realization. In this way Christ's word about the nearness of the kingdom of God already contains an anticipation of God's dominion over man and things; devil and sin, illness and death, which so long dominated man and nature are deprived of their power and in their place comes the dominion of God. A miracle shows that the preaching is no idle word, but a deed of God. On the other hand the word reveals the true character of the miracle, which in itself is open to various interpretations. Christ pointed out this active character of the revelation he brought and he connected the miracles with the coming of the kingdom of God: "But if it is by the Spirit of God that I cast out demons, then the kingdom of God has come upon you" (Mt. 11:28=Lk. 11:20). "Now . . . John . . . sent word by his disciples and said to him: Are you he who is to come, or shall we look for another? And Jesus answered them: Go and tell John what you hear and see: the blind receive their sight and the lame walk, lepers are cleansed and the deaf hear, and the dead are raised up, and the poor have good news preached to them" (Mt. 11:2-5=Lk. 7:18-22, with reference to Is. 35:5-6; 61-1).

Man's response to this preaching of the kingdom of God is belief of the word. The necessity of this faith is not removed because people see revelation by deed in the miracles: both the deed and the word of Christ demand a decision from man. The sign itself is not compelling enough to demand man's decision. When Jesus summed up the series of miracles which legitimized his preaching of the kingdom of God, he added significantly: "Blessed is he who takes no offense at me" (Mt. 11:6=Lk. 7:23). Faith must be accompanied by conversion and turning back. Man with his entire being must turn away from all that militates against God and his dominion, and resolutely turn to God with a perfect openness and obedience (Mt. 4:17=Mk. 1:13; cf. Lk. 5:32).

The revelation of the mysteries of the kingdom. Besides this preaching, revelation of God's kingdom by word and deed, there is a revelation which penetrates deeper into the essence of the kingdom. In it the element of knowledge is important and Jesus' intimate disciples are the ones who listen to it. Here we meet the important word "mystery": "And he answered them: To you it has been given to know the secrets of the kingdom of heaven, but to them it has not been given" (Mt. 13:11=Lk. 8:10, ff.; cf. Mk. 4:11 where the aspect of knowledge is not used: "To you has been given the secret of the kingdom of God, but for those outside everything is in parables"). Thus we are taken back to the apocalyptic phase which attached great importance to the revelation and the knowledge of mysteries. Here we must consider the book of Daniel, where knowledge of the kingdom and its history and evolution belong to the mysteries concerning the end time, revealed by God in visions (cf. Dan. 2:28-29).

In this context of mystery revelations we should place some of the parables (cf. 13:3-9, 18-23; 13:24-30, 36-43), which in a hidden way reveal the essence of the kingdom of God to some extent and thus constitute a primary level in the knowledge of the "mysteries." But as a normal and necessary complement they need further explanation, just as the parable visions of the apocalyptics must be supplemented by an interpretation (the dreams or visions of the king, interpreted by Daniel; the visions of Daniel himself, explained by an angel). We cannot here undertake an explanation of the essence of the kingdom of God from the parables. We merely wish to show their central role in this intellectual revelation concerning the kingdom of heaven.

The revelation of the Father and the Son. Progressive revelation about the essence of the kingdom is important; so too is that given to the disciples about their king, Christ. We will not dwell too long on some texts attributable to the earthly Jesus where he professes to be the Son of Man coming on the clouds of heaven (Mt. 26:64=Mk. 14:62; cf. Lk. 22:60). There is another passage of greater theological depth; it is placed explicitly within the framework of revelational terminology and evidently shows the influence of the "Son of Man" view. This text, because of great similarity with some of John's statements about Christ is known as the "Joannine word" (**logion Johanneum**). It sheds a clear light on the personal relationship of Jesus with the Father: "At the same time Jesus declared: I thank thee, Father, Lord of heaven and earth, that thou hast hidden these things from the wise and understanding and revealed them to babes; yes Father, for so it was well-pleasing before thee. All things have been delivered to me by my Father, and no one knows the Son except the Father, and no one knows the Father except the Son and any one to whom the Son chooses to reveal him" (Mt. 11:25-27=Lk. 10:21-22).

The main point of this text is the verse which mentions the revelation of the Father by the Son. Here the Father is so hidden and inaccessible that knowledge of his being — that is to say, perfect knowledge — is accessible only to Jesus, the Son. Jesus claims for himself a divine knowledge which presupposes his own divine being. This essential equality of Son and Father is also expressed by "All things have been delivered to me by my Father." This "delivering all things" to the Son approaches, in form and content, close to the proclamation of his universal dominion by which the Risen Christ (Mt. 28:18) introduces and establishes the mission of the apostles; it is also close to the attribution of eschatological judicial power John ascribes to Christ in Jn. 5:22, 27. Here again we return to the text of Daniel where God gives the Son of Man an imperishable kingdom (Dan. 7:13-14). If this text means that universal power is given to Christ, meaning of the all-encompassing "**all things** (are delivered to me)" is not yet exhausted. Remaining within the context of Daniel we may say that these "delivered things" include the mysteries of the kingdom and of God.

It is one and the same God who gives the kingdom
to the Son of Man (Dan. 7:13-14) and who reveals
mysteries to his prophet (Dan. 2:20-23; 30:47). Therefore Jesus can reveal the mystery of God himself
(cf. also the word about the mysteries of the kingdom
of God, which in the version of Mk. is rendered
as giving the mystery **itself** in the version of Mt. and
Lk. as giving the **knowledge** of the mystery).

The "Joannine word" presents, in addition to the
revelation about the Father, a self-revelation of
Christ, as regards his divine nature and his oneness
with the Father and his function as a mediator of
revelation for man.

The perfect equality of the Son with the Father
implies that only the Father can reveal Jesus as the
Son, a conclusion succintly affirmed in the introductory verse: "Thou hast revealed them to babes"
(11:25). Matthew underlines this idea in the famous
Peter text (Mt. 16:13-19), where the parallel between
"Son of Man" (verse 13) and "Son of the living God"
(verse 16) explains Peter's confession of faith in the
sense of an utterance about Christ's divine nature,
knowledge of which could only have been given by
the Father: "And Jesus answered him: Blessed are
you, Simon Bar-Jona! For flesh and blood has not
revealed this to you, but my Father who is in heaven"
(verse 17).

But Christ still remains hidden, even to his most
intimate disciples. This is indicated when he reveals his future suffering and death to the twelve.

The same Peter, whose confession of faith was ascribed by Christ to a revelation of the Father, objects to this revelation of the suffering Messiah, showing the stupidity of one who does not think like God and must hear from Christ the terrible words: "Get behind me, satan!" (Mt. 16:21-23=Mk. 8:31-33; cf. Lk. 9:44-45; 18:31-34). The disciples, it is true, are ready to accept a Christ in glory, but they refuse the revelation of Jesus as the Suffering Servant of God, who in a prophetic reference to his future death founds the New Testament in his blood (cf. Lk. 22:15-20, 24-27, 35-38).

This blindness of the disciples to the revelation about the suffering is further enhanced by an event which should have opened their eyes: the fulfillment of Jesus' prophetic word at his death (Lk. 24:5-11). It is removed only by a revealing act of God, which excludes any doubt: Christ is raised from the dead.

The resurrection as eschatological revelation. To gain a better insight in the revelational importance of the resurrection we must first consider it in itself, before its announcement to the group of privileged disciples. New Testament writings consider the resurrection as such to be the supremely great revealing deed. God, raising Christ from the dead, performs an action which begins the end time in the strict sense; his divine dominion irrevocably takes control (cf. however the special view of John!). The miraculous signs of the earthly Christ, such as the cures or even the raising of the dead to life constituted an anticipation of the kingdom of God, of his dominion over sin, illness and death. But in these miracles the kingdom of God appeared only in a relative sense; practically, death kept its power over all who for a short time were snatched from his dominion. The resurrection of Christ however is accomplished on a totally different level; it introduces him into this glory, the glory of God himself: "Was it not necessary that the Christ should suffer these things and enter into his glory?" (Lk. 24:26). Now Christ once for all is taken away from death, which constituted the power of sin and the devil; he, and only he, is the firstling of those who must rise from the sleep of death (1 Cor. 15:20, 23); in him God's dominion emerges triumphant. This necessarily will achieve its final completion by the resurrection of the faithful on the day when the Son of Man is revealed as Lord of the entire world (Lk. 17:30; cf. Mt. 13:36-43; 24:30-31). When the Risen One proclaims in Mt. 28:18-20: "All authority in heaven and on earth has been given to me," and sends his disciples over the entire world in order to actually realize this dominion, or when in Lk. 24:47 he gives a similar command, we see in them the conviction that with the resurrection of Christ and his glorification the dominion of God himself begins to realize itself irrevocably (cf. especially 1 Cor. 15:25-28).

Since Christ is vested with the glory of God himself by his resurrection, we must not be surprised that in this revealing deed an aspect of mystery prevails, more than in any other Biblical revealing act;

that is why the canonical gospels significantly do not describe the resurrection itself. By this act Christ is received into the mystery of God and this revelation by deed requires a new revealing act on God's part so that this secret be revealed to the witnesses he had chosen. The revealing of the Risen One takes place in his apparitions. Christ here comes out of his hidden abode with God, in a manner in which the visual element prevails: "He appeared" (Lk. 24:34; Mt. 28:7, 10; Mk. 16:7). In the risen body of the Crucified One the eschatological dominion and glory of God was unmistakably revealed to the eye-witnesses.

Testimony and tradition. The revelation of the risen Christ now becomes the starting point of a tradition through witnesses. The contents of this tradition are partly indicated at the end of the gospel of Luke (24:44-49) and the corresponding introduction of Acts (1:3-8): the Risen One gives the eye-witnesses of his apparitions the mission to testify about his salutary death and resurrection; it teaches also the meaning ascribed to it by his own prophetic word and by Scriptural prophecies. He himself, by his resurrection — and we may add, by his Spirit (Lk. 24:40) — opens to his disciples the deeper sense of the Scriptures and of his own prophetic words. When Matthias is chosen as an apostle, Peter points out that the contents of tradition concern also the ministry of Christ; this he does by insisting, a necessary condition, that the candidate must have seen the risen Christ and that he, together with the twelve, has accompanied Jesus during his preaching: "So one of the men who have accompanied us during all the time that the Lord Jesus went in and out among us, beginning from the baptism of John until the day when he was taken up from us — one of these men must become with us a witness to his resurrection" (Acts 1:21-22).

The word "tradition" is not found in these quotations, but that this testimony actually is traditional, appears from the prologue of Luke's gospel, which very compactly describes the whole process which begins with the eye and ear-witnesses, is formulated in the oral tradition or preaching of the word, and finally finds its expression in Scripture: "Inasmuch as many have undertaken to complete a narrative of the things which have been accomplished among us, just as they were delivered to us by those who from the beginning were eye-witnesses and ministers of the word" (Lk. 1:1-2). "Testimony" adds to "tradition" a unique personal experience of what is testified, and over above this the personal engagement of the witness.

The texts amply show that this tradition in a very special way also includes the deeds of Jesus during his earthly existence and the words he had spoken about his being sent, his nature, about following him, etc. From the form of some words or sayings (especially if we translate them back from Greek into Aramaic, the mother tongue of Christ) which are still to be found in the gospels, and especially from their parallelism and rhythm, from allusions, alliterations and nuances we can gather that Jesus in several cases used the methods of tradition current in Judaism (cf. Mt. 6:9-13; 11:17). We must however add that even this is not enough to prove that those words already had this form in the oral instruction of Jesus himself or received it only in the oral tradition of the apostles. Jesus himself had very strongly opposed the doctrine of the pharisees and scribes and stigmatized it in its excesses as a "tradition of men" (Mt. 15:1-9=Mk. 7:1-13). Nevertheless he acted like a rabbi when he formulated his new and authoritative doctrine in such a way that it could easily be handed down by oral tradition and that it thus must have shown the features listed above.

And yet, if we study the Gospels closely we see that the earthly Jesus, though he used the technique of rabbinic methods in handing down his message, usually did not do so in the fixed manner customary with schooled rabbis. We find a most striking example in two such essential expressions as the prayer he himself taught his disciples and the formula he used when he instituted the New Covenant in his blood. Both the text of the Our Father (Mt. 6:9-13; Lk. 11:2-4) and the eucharistic formula (Mt. 26:26-28; Lk. 22:19-20) have been handed down to us in different forms, with differences that probably existed already at the level of oral tradition. Various influences have acted on this tradition; as a result, the words and deeds of Jesus have not kept their strictly original form. This process has also continued on the level of the written tradition, as the evangelists more than once, under the influence of theological and other motives, changed the words and deeds that (orally or by writing) had been handed down to them.

Here we encounter facts which in a more or less decisive way raise the problem of continuity between the historical Jesus and the Christ of apostolic preaching. Here we can only indicate the problem, because we are sure that the objective solution which shall be given to it cannot be contrary to the promise of Christ when he sent his apostles to go and preach his message.

2

THE LETTERS OF PAUL

The vision of the apostle's vocation. A very personal and extraordinary revelation stands at the beginning of Paul's Christian life; this essentially determines his preaching and his theology. In his controversy with the Galatians, who were in danger of losing their faith, he gives a concise but at the same time a complete account of the divine origin and of the contents of his preaching: "But when he who had set me apart before I was born, and had called me through his grace, was pleased to reveal his Son to me, in order that I might preach him among the gentiles, I did not confer with flesh and blood" (1:15-16).

Some scholars have rightly pointed out the great resemblance of this revelation which Paul received with the revelation Peter received according to the gospel of Matthew (Mt. 16:13-19). In both cases the revelation comes directly from God, not from man ("flesh and blood"); in both cases it lays the foundation for a unique mission (cf. Gal. 2:7-8); and finally the theme in both cases is God's own Son. We may assume that this means, in the letter to the Galatians — as well as in the pericope of

Matthew — a revelation about Jesus' divine nature:
when Paul speaks about God's Son, he has in mind
Christ's pre-existence with the Father, whose nature
he shares (cf. Gal. 4:4; Rom. 1:3; 8:3; Phil. 2:6-7).
But the revelational content of the Pauline text expresses more than only this. The Son of God is the
pre-existing One who, after dying, was glorified by
God. Paul sees in the Son of God first of all and in
fullness the "Son of God in power," who in the resurrection was exalted to be the Lord of glory (Rom.
1:4). This we see perhaps even more clearly in the
second letter to the Corinthians, where Paul again
has to defend the authority of his apostolate against
the fanaticism of his Jewish antagonists and describes
the Damascus vision with these words: "For it is
the God who said: Let light shine out of darkness,
who has shone in our hearts to give the light of the
knowledge of the glory of God in the face of Christ"
(4:6). Before the gates of Damascus the risen Christ
appeared to the apostle in a dazzling light and
touched his heart inwardly (cf. Acts 9:1-9).

Here we are taught too that the revelation of the
Son at the same time implies self-revelation of God.
God's own glory shines over the face of Christ: in
the risen Lord the image of God himself becomes
visible to us (cf. 2 Cor. 3:18; 4:4; Rom. 8:29-30; Col.
1:15).

This divine revelation became intellectually accessible to Paul as an object of knowledge; at the same
time it was a deed of God, intending to change the
apostle. The revelation of God's Son brought him

from the darkness of sin to the light of God's glory; the manifestation of the Risen One to Paul was his vocation to salvation. He was seized by Christ. Only after having in this way more or less understood what this vision of Paul meant for his vocation can we understand how he could describe the Son of God as a theme of the good news, "in order that I might preach him among the gentiles."

We must look again at the last part of this text. By mentioning the destination of Paul's preaching it signalizes the uniqueness of his gospel as compared to the gospel of the other apostles, especially of Peter: "He who worked through Peter for the mission to the circumcised, worked through me also for the gentiles" (Gal. 2:8). This specification of Paul's mission grace perhaps is hinted at when Paul speaks about "my gospel" (Rom. 2:16; 16:25). However this expression may be understood in the letters of captivity, it is a fact that the gentiles are received within the contents of "mystery," which then largely replaces the former "gospel."

The preaching of the gospel as revelation. In the text of Gal. 1:15-16, hitherto the main object of our meditations, revelation was understood as taking place in Paul himself: "He . . . was pleased to reveal his Son to me." From this exposition we could not conclude what kind of revelation the ensuing preaching was to be. To obtain a deeper insight into this matter we must turn to the letter to the Romans. This writing, though it has many content similarities with Galatians usually is less controversial in its tone, more inviting or even comtemplative.

The letter as a whole centers around the description and deepening of the essence of the good news and we may see it summarized in the topical verses: "For I am not ashamed of the gospel: it is the power of God for salvation to every one who has faith, to the Jew first and also to the Greek. For in it the righteousness of God is revealed through faith for faith; as it is written: He who through faith is righteous shall live" (1:16-17). Here the kerygma — the preaching itself — is described as a milieu for revelation: in the gospel preaching God's justice is manifested (cf. Rom. 3:21-26). This revelation also is being enacted on a twofold level. First it addresses the intellect and the will. The preacher directs the good news to everybody; the atoning death and resurrection of Christ has revealed man's radical sinfulness, and God's plan for the sinner. Not wrath but love is his last word: he will give salvation in Christ, he will show the sinner his saving justice, his divine qualities of fidelity, truth and mercy. This manifestation or revelation of the divine saving will, hitherto hidden from man, does not become an actual reality unless the hearer himself speaks his "yes" to God's saving mercy. But as soon as man has assented, God's justice becomes real and powerful in him: the gospel, the preaching of God's Son in power, turns into a real manifestation of God's forgiving and sanctifying justice. The circumcision of the heart, which could not be brought about by the economy of law, now is brought about by the Holy Spirit, the salutary gift of the New Testament, announced by the prophets (Rom. 2:20;

2 Cor. 3:3, 6; cf. Jer. 31:31-34; Ezek. 36:26-27). Thus among Christians the demands of the law and the holy will of God (Rom. 8:4; 7:12) summarized as love for God and fellowman (13:8-10), are fulfilled in virtue of the Spirit of love (5:5; 8:2, 4, 14-16).

What the topical verses of Rom. 1:16-17 have mentioned as salvation and justification we may in another way also describe (cf. 3:23) as a manifestation of God's glory, in accord with the thought content of the above quotation from the second letter to the Corinthians: "And we all, with unveiled face, reflecting the glory of the Lord, are being changed into his likeness from one degree of glory to another" (3:18).

We have a familiar commentary on Gen. 15:6 in Rom. 4; here continuous references to Abraham's example shed light from various sides on man's reaction to preaching. This response comprises almost all positive human actions found in the various parts of the Old Testament. It is a confiding faith, based, against all human expectations, on divine omnipotence and goodness: "In hope he believed against hope, that he should become the father of many nations" (4:18). Faith as such allows God to be God, it gives him the honor and praise due only to him: "He gave glory to God, fully convinced that God was able to do what he had promised" (4:20-21). Since it is an action of a sinner who knows that he is guilty before his Creator, it also includes conversion to him: "And to one who does not work but trusts him who justifies the ungodly, his faith reckoned as righteousness" (4:5). One factor, not mentioned in this passage — outward confession of faith — will be mentioned further on in the same letter in an allusion to the baptismal liturgy: "Because, if you confess with your lips that Jesus is Lord and believe in your heart that God raised him from the dead, you will be saved. For man believes with his heart and so is justified, and he confesses with his lips and so is saved" (10:9-10).

Thus one continuous line connects the Old and the New Covenant: the main difference is that the God, who calls the dead to life, in this end time has definitively and exclusively revealed himself in the person of Jesus Christ.

Speaking about the revelation of God's justice in the good news the letter to the Romans also touches on the problem of the revelation by creation: "For what can be known about God is plain to them, because God has shown it to them. Ever since the creation of the world his invisible nature, namely, his eternal power and deity, has been clearly perceived in the things that have been made" (1:19-20). As elsewhere so also here Paul's vision cannot be expressed in a simple "yes" or "no": the position he adopts is so many-sided that it implies both a refusal and an approval. New Testament revelation pronounces its verdict on the real deformation which the knowledge of God, drawn from the revelation by creation, took on in pagan idolatry. The pagans are without excuse because "by their wickedness they suppress the truth (about God)" and because "although they knew God they did not honor him as God or give thanks to him," but "exchanged the glory of the immortal God for idols" (1:20, 21, 23). But following the example of hellenistic Judaism and linking it with stoic theological reasoning (1:19-20), Paul explicitly indicates the knowledge of God hidden under this idolatrous deformation. He approves of the natural knowledge of God which in stoic philosophy had partially freed itself from its actual deterioration into idolatry and was on its way to knowledge of the true God. By the light of the special revelation, present in Israel and in Christ, he brings the natural knowledge of God, ultimately based on a general revelation by creation, back to the pure condition it originally had by God's intention; thus it again becomes a positive starting point for Christian preaching.[18]

The revelation of the mystery. Paul ends his letter to the Romans, dedicated to God's revelation in the gospel, with magnificent praise of God: "Now to him who is able to strengthen you according to my gospel and the preaching of Jesus Christ, according to the revelation of the mystery which was kept secret for long ages but is now disclosed and through the prophetic writings is made known to all nations, according to the command of the eternal God, to bring about the obedience of faith — to the only wise God be glory for evermore through Jesus Christ. Amen" (16:25-27). In this hymn, rich in theological thought, the preaching of the gospel is presented as a revelation of "the mystery." Thus we encounter a notion which increasingly is to dominate Paul's thinking about revelation. While the synoptic gospels refer the mysteries to the kingdom of God, Paul sees them in their deepest sense as essentially connected with Christ's person and the Church, and thus expressing God's all embracing plan of salvation. As such this notion can be found, though in the form of a kind of adjectival description in 1 Cor. 2:7 ("secret and hidden wisdom of God"). Though the term "mystery" has been introduced in Rom. 11:25-26 (in conjunction with sapiential terminology in 11: 33-35), it appears only at the end of Romans (16:25-27); not before Colossians (1:26-27; 2:2; 4:3) and Ephesians (1:9; 3:3-4, 9; 6:19) does it reach its full extension. In the pastoral letters it comes to the fore in important texts (1 Tim. 3:16; cf. 3:9).

That mystery is connected with revelation appears from the many revelational terms with which it is used, such as: revelation (Rom. 16:25; Eph. 3:3), revealing (1 Cor. 2:10; Eph. 3:5), manifesting (Rom. 16:26; Col. 1:26; 4:4), making known (Rom. 16:26; Eph. 1:9; 3:5, 10; Col. 1:27), bringing to the light (Eph. 3:9).

This identification with revelational terms is not at all strange, for a first quality of a mystery is its secrecy. God had from all eternity conceived the plan of salvation concerning mankind and creation but "the mystery . . . was kept secret for long ages" (Rom. 16:25), not only from the "other generations" (Eph. 3:5; Col. 1:26), but even from the heavenly spirit (Eph. 3:9-10).

However it did not remain hidden in God. Old Testament prophetic preaching was a faint light announcing the approaching dawn (Rom. 16:26). But the real revelation comes only in the eschatological "now" of Christian times (Rom. 16:25; Col. 1:26). The privileged mediators of this revelation are the apostles and the New Testament prophets to whom the mystery was directly revealed:". . . which was not made known to the sons of men in other generations as it has now been revealed to his holy apostles and prophets by the Spirit" (Eph. 3:5). But as founders of the Church (Eph. 2:10) and as first "gifts" of the glorified Christ (4:12) they receive the task of announcing the mystery to others in their turn (cf. 3:2, 8-10).

The eschatological "now" by which the period of revelation is inaugurated begins, according to 1 Tim. 3:16, with the incarnation of Christ (cf. 2 Tim. 1:10; Tit. 2:11; 3:4). But according to the general trend of Paul's letters it reaches its height only with the death and resurrection of Christ (Eph. 1:7-9). Therefore the mystery according to 1 Cor. 2:6-16 may be identified with the crucified Lord of glory. Although Christ always remains the center of salvation, the aspects under which this mystery is considered are developed and become broader.

Thus in Colossians the mystery is "Christ among us," ". . . the mystery hidden for ages and generations but now made manifest to his saints. To them God chose to make known how great among the gentiles are the riches of the glory of this mystery, which is Christ in you, the hope of glory" (1:26-27).[19]

Ephesians brings further development; here the Church made up of Jews and pagans is presented as the mystery of Christ's Body. As to the manifestation of the depths of this concept a privileged position, unique among all the apostles, must be assigned to Paul: "When you read this you can perceive my insight into the mystery of Christ, which was not made known to the sons of men in other generations as it has now been revealed to his holy apostles and prophets by the Spirit; that is, how the gentiles are fellow heirs, members of the same body, and partakers of the promise in Christ Jesus through the gospel. Of this gospel I was made a minister according to the gift of God's grace which was given me by the working of his power. To me, though I am the very least of all the saints, this grace was given, to preach to the gentiles the unsearchable riches of Christ, and to make all men see what is the plan of the mystery hidden for ages" (Eph. 3:4-9a).

The mystery in this letter is not limited to earthly dimensions; it assumes the immeasurable dimensions of the universe, including the heavenly powers. God before all times directed the heavenly powers — here called "ages" — toward Christ and the Church. He has moreover decided ". . . to unite all things in him, things in heaven and things on earth" (1:10). Christ himself in this way is the Head and the summation of all creatures by being the Head of the Church; through the Church, his Body and his

fullness, he assumes the universe within himself
and subjects it: "And he has put all things under his
feet and had made him the head over all things
for the Church, which is his body, the fullness of
him who fills all in all" (1:22-23).

We cannot stress the cosmic dimensions of the
mystery in Ephesians strongly enough; the same
can be said of the universal role ascribed there to
the Church as the place and content of revelation
— creation, redemption, and last things, even in a
certain sense Christ himself are all referred to the
Church, seen as the realization of the mystery revealed by God. This in its fullness is made known
by the Church's preaching as well as in the entire
essence of the Church itself: "The mystery (was) for
ages hidden in God who created all things; that
through the Church the manifold wisdom of God
might now be made known to the principalities and
powers in the heavenly places" (3:9b-10).

The revelation of the gospel, as described in
Romans, was a manifestation of the operation of the
justice of God; the revelation of the mystery however,
in which the intellectual aspect is accentuated, is
seen as a presentation of divine wisdom, personified
in Christ and existent in the Church (cf. Eph. 3:9b-10;
2 Cor. 1:23-24, 30; 2:6-8; Rom. 16:27; Col. 1:13-20;
2:2-3; text to be compared with the Old Testament
passages about personified wisdom).

The mystery as such is destined to be the object
of an ever deeper contemplation. It is accepted in

faith, but is only fully realized in a deeper knowledge or **gnosis** of faith, to such an extent that understanding it becomes the distinguishing feature and the center of Christian life.

In communicating this knowledge, which penetrates into the depths of God and his plan of salvation contained in the mystery, the Holy Spirit plays an indispensible role, because he alone, as the Spirit of God, can gauge the depths of God: ". . . in my prayers, that the God of our Lord Jesus Christ may give you a spirit of wisdom and of revelation in the knowledge of him, having the eyes of your heart enlightened, that you may know what is the hope to which he has called you, what are the riches of his glorious inheritance in the saints, and what is the immeasurable greatness of his power in us who believe" (Eph. 1:17-19a).[20] Every Christian is called to perfection gained by an evolving understanding of the mystery; it is the normal development comparable to natural growth to maturity (Col. 1:28; Eph. 4:12-13). But this supposes that in his moral life he allowed himself to be led by the Spirit (Rom. 8:12-16; 1 Cor. 2:14; 3:4). Knowledge of God's salvation plan is accompanied by an ever increasing love (cf. Col. 2:2-3; Eph. 3:16-19).

Eschatological revelation and glorification of God. In reading the captivity letters there would seem to be no denying that, because of the ever increasing conviction of an already realized eschatology, present contemplation of the mystery is so highly valued that the strictly eschatological realities seemingly fade into the background. Nevertheless this revelation and the corresponding knowledge of the faith are only stages on the road to the final revelation. Contemplation, during our life time, remains entirely within the boundaries of faith (Rom. 1:17). The object of the mystery is the Lord of glory (1 Cor. 2:8). God has destined this mystery for our glorification (1 Cor. 2:7; Col. 1:27). But both his glory and ours, which is only a sharing in his (2 Cor. 3:18), are accessible only by faith, not by immediate vision (1 Cor. 13:12; 2 Cor. 5:7). The final goal of Christian life still remains the revelation of our Lord Jesus Christ at his return (2 Thess. 1:7; 1 Cor. 1:7) and, simultaneously, the revelation of the glory of God's children and of creation: "I consider that the sufferings of the present time are not worth comparing to the glory that is to be revealed to us. For the creation waits with eager longing for the revealing of the sons of God . . . because the creation itself will be set free from its bondage to decay and obtain the glorious liberty of the children of God" (Rom. 8:18-19, 21; cf. Col. 3:4).

Only then the the final aim of revelation shall be reached. This is the glorification of God, as it has been sung in hymns which are only a faint anticipation of the praise the entire creation will one day sing in the last manifestation of the mystery. Then God, through Christ and the Church, shall be all in all (Eph. 1:3-14; Rom. 11:33-35; 16:25-27).

Paul and tradition. Paul received his intellectual education at the feet of rabbi Gamaliel (Acts 22:3).

He was educated by scribes, whose ideal was receiving and accurately transmitting the "traditions
of the fathers" (Gal. 1:14). Hence one is not surprised
to find him using the vocabulary associated with the
Jewish notion of tradition; this incidentally shows
striking similarities with the "traditions" in the
philosophy and mystery religions of hellenism: transmitting, tradition, holding fast (the three terms in 1
Cor. 11:2; cf. 2 Thess. 2:15), receiving (1 Cor. 11:23).

But this similarity in form also obscures a real
difference of content and authority.

The content of the tradition the apostle handed
down to the communities is what, in another context
and under another aspect, is presented as the object
of revelation: the good news, the gospel he himself
has "received by a revelation of Jesus Christ" (Gal.
1:11-12). In the terminology of the captivity letters:
"Christ Jesus, the Lord . . . the mystery of God . . .
in whom are hid all the treasures of wisdom and
knowledge" (Col. 2:2; 3:6).

The death and resurrection of Christ, as always,
remain the central points of the gospel tradition. In
transmitting these realities the apostle knows that
he is immediately dependent on the risen Christ, who
appeared to him near Damascus (Gal. 1:11-12, 15-17).
This however does not prevent him from giving these
truths, in the first letter to the Corinthians, a formulation which, according to his own words, was borrowed from a tradition which ultimately must have
originated in some way from the apostles of Jeru-

salem: "For I delivered to you as of first importance what I also received, that Christ died for our sins in accordance with the Scriptures, that he was buried, that he was raised on the third day in accordance with the Scriptures, and that he appeared to Cephas, then to the twelve" (15:3-5).

We must point out that the contents of the tradition in this case are not quite the same as the risen Christ's revelation to Paul; this traditional formula also contains items which Paul in last resort evidently learned only by the testimony of the twelve — the resurrection of Christ on the third day and his appearance to Peter and the twelve. Paul's personal revelation agrees with and confirms the preaching of the first witnesses, just as his preaching is confirmed and supplemented by theirs.

It is in keeping with the theme of Colossians, where Christ is proclaimed Lord over all cosmic powers, that he is also designated as the object of tradition: "As therefore you received Christ Jesus the Lord, so live in him, rooted and built up in him and established in the faith, just as you were taught, abounding in thanksgiving. See to it that no one makes a prey of you by philosophy and empty deceit, according to human tradition, according to the elemental spirits of the universe, and not according to Christ" (2:6-9). Evidently the letter here assumes the terminology of the erring teachers to whom "philosophy" was "handed over" in a mysterious initiation. Paul deprecates this by the expression, "human tradition." The divine revelation of the mystery concerns Christ, and only him "in whom are hid all the treasures of wisdom and knowledge" (2:3). This was handed down to the Colossians by the preachers of the faith. In baptism Christians accepted and acknowledged Christ as the "Lord."

Besides this tradition, which has as its direct object the person of Christ who died and rose and was established as Lord over the creation, the vocabulary of tradition is also used for certain rules determining the moral attitude of the individual Christian or discipline within the community. These rules too are "tradition" and have complete authority.

We meet an example which stands on the boundary between these in 1 Corinthians: "For I received from the Lord what I also delivered to you, that the Lord Jesus on the night when he was betrayed took bread, and when he had given thanks, he broke it and said: This is my body which is for you. Do this in remembrance of me. In the same way also the cup, after supper, saying: This cup is the New Covenant in my blood. Do this, as often as you drink it, in remembrance of me" (11:23-25). Insofar as these words show a method for celebrating the Eucharist according to the model of the Lord's Supper, and are at the same time intended to check existing abuses in the community, they are transmitted "rules." But on the other hand this tradition again touches the very heart of the good news, insofar as, by way of liturgical action, it announces the death of Christ (11:26) by which the new and eternal covenant between God and men has been made. In any event, rejection of such a tradition would be contrary to God's explicit will, because it has its ultimate origin in Christ: "For I received from the Lord what I also delivered to you." The content and the formulation of this tradition, as well as the Greek preposition used here, point to the fact that the apostle did not receive the tradition directly from the earthly Christ, nor from the risen Christ personally, nor by being present at the Last Supper in some idealistic or mystic way; it reached him through human transmitters. He appeals to the authority of the Lord, but in this case only indirectly. This text is important because it supplies us with a clear example of Paul's dependence on apostolic tradition for facts or words concerning the earthly Christ, about which he had no knowledge from his vision near Damascus nor from later revelations. Some scholars, it is true, have believed that this and similar formulas, in which Paul ascribes a rule to the Lord (cf. 1 Cor. 7:10), may be explained as if the apostle would appeal to the glorified Christ himself, who directly from heaven, is speaking in the historical tradition. Now there can be no doubt that Paul considers himself as an apostle in immediate contact with the glorified Christ, and that on this account he can give admonitions and rules (1 Cor. 7:40), or interpret and adapt transmitted formulas of faith (cf. the formulas which are the basis of Rom. 1:3-4 and Phil. 2:5-11). None the less, the text of 1 Cor. 11:23-25 (and 1 Cor. 7:10) must be interpreted without recurring to the glorified Christ for an answer. We find this explanation of a historical tradition with its train of transmitters, and of the direct activity of the heavenly Lord in the last period of Paul's life; this we will now consider.

The idea of tradition plays an important role in the letters written at the end of Paul's life, the so-called pastoral letters addressed to Timothy and Titus. Even if they should have been written only by his orders, and if the vocabulary should not come directly from him, they still can be considered presenting his views.

At the time when he had to reckon earnestly with his approaching death an important evolution of his view on the tradition took place. Until then he himself had stood in the center of the process. It was he who transmitted the traditions to his communities, even though he sometimes sent a pupil to remind them of his "ways in Christ" (1 Cor. 4:17). Now he formulates the principle of succession in tradition. He and his personal testimony are going to disappear, but the tradition of this testimony goes on unobstructed and infallibly, until the end. His immediate successor is found in the person and the ministry of Timothy: "But I am not ashamed, for I know whom I have believed, and I am sure that he is able to guard until that day what has been entrusted to me (literally: the deposit). Follow the pattern of the sound words which you have heard from me, in the faith and love which are in Christ Jesus: guard the truth that has been entrusted to you (literally: the deposit) by the Holy Spirit who dwells within us" (2 Tim. 1:12-14). It seems to us that Paul, in referring to the "sound words" Timothy has heard from him — the preaching of the gospel — no longer uses the words "transmitting" and "receiving." Instead of the different "traditions" he now speaks about the "deposit." In this word there is unmistakable emphasis on the treasure to be transmitted. The author here applies a juridical term to Christian preaching, when it was threatened with falsification by erring teachers. Just as in business law the entrusted deposit had to be faithfully guarded and returned intact to the possessor, so also Timothy must — like Paul — keep intact for the sake of God the doctrine entrusted to him.

With this thought of guarding the deposit a companion reality is introduced by the fact that charism is mentioned. This is confirmed if we compare the quoted text with 1 Tim. 6:20 where the admonition "to guard" the deposit comes at the end of the admonition concerning ordination (1 Tim. 6:11-16). Guarding the deposit has been made possible by the Spirit; the charism in its turn is given by the "laying on of hands": "Hence I remind you to rekindle the gift of God that is within you through the laying on of my hands; for God did not give us a spirit of timidity but a spirit of power and love and self-control" (2 Tim. 1:6-7). Thus the faithful keeping of tradition is linked with the office. This office itself knows a train of succession; Paul, reckoning with the eventuality of Timothy's death, invites him: "What you have heard from me before many witnesses entrust to faithful men who will be able to teach others also" (2 Tim. 2:2).

Summarizing, we can sketch the following train of traditions: Christ — Paul — the apostle's pupil Timothy — the trustworthy men, to be identified with the "elders" or **presbyteroi** (Tit. 1:5-6). Thus tradition includes a historical succession of transmitters, who empirically establish a link with the apostles and the Christ of history; in and through this succession is also included a permanent vertical contact with the glorified Christ through the Spirit.

The Holy Spirit is first seen as the power of the grace received at ordination; this enables the ordained man to hand down to successors in the office the entrusted deposit of faith: "You then, my son, be strong in the grace that is in Christ Jesus, and what you have heard . . . entrust" (2 Tim. 2:1-2). But it would be strange indeed if the creating Spirit would only lend himself to a literal, strict and almost mechanical repetition and tradition of the doctrine of faith! The Spirit should rather be seen as the one who, together with fidelity to the doctrine, also supplies the power of evolving the message according to the variable needs of the times. This is sufficiently indicated by the text in 2 Tim. 1:12-14. It should be noted here that the Greek word **hypotyposis** in our translation is rendered by "pattern" (norm, model). In profane life this term indicated a sculptured or painted design awaiting further finishing and completion; it also designated a summary giving a general idea of a topic, but not yet a complete exposition. Applied to tradition this means that Timothy and his successors shall not content themselves with merely repeating the words directly or indirectly received from Paul; on the contrary, they must by themselves develop, actualize and apply the transmitted doctrine, led by the vivifying Spirit of Christ who, owing to the apostolic succession, is present at every moment and on behalf of every moment.

3

THE WRITINGS OF JOHN

This survey is dedicated to those writings of the New Testament which usually are called "Joannine." We may assuredly accept the view that all these writings ultimately originated from one and the same great personality; nevertheless, we prefer, because of the different genres, to deal with Revelation separately from the Gospel and the letters.

The Apocalypse or Revelation. As is obvious from this title, there is among John's writings a book which differs from all the other New Testament writings in that it explicitly and in its entirety professes to be a "revelation." The introductory verses say: "The revelation of Jesus Christ, which God gave him to show to his servants what must soon take place; and he made it known by sending his angel to his servant John, who bore witness to the word of God and to the testimony of Jesus Christ, even to all that he saw. Blessed is he who reads aloud the words of the prophecy and blessed are those who hear, and who keep what is written down therein; for the time is near" (1:1-3).

Here we have a "revelation of Jesus Christ"; the explanatory words "which God gave to him" show

that John meant a revelation which has Jesus Christ
as its chief mediator. The Father has communicated
his hidden mysteries to the Son of Man, that he in
his turn should reveal them to his servants — the
prophets. In these verses John at the same time
indicates the way he received the revelation of
Christ: "all that he **saw**" therefore by means of visions.
If we read the visions of Revelation we see that a
distinguishing mark in them is their frequent sym-
bolism. Such means of revealing — as well as their
contents — place this revelation in the theological
sphere and literary genre of apocalyptic writings.
This is true to the extent that John's book, being
pre-eminently **the** apocalypse, later gave its name
to the whole class of writings. Unlike the majority
of Jewish apocalyptic visions which were only
literary fictions and owed their origin to the religious
fancy of pietistic people, the Apocalypse of John is
the result of a real revelation. The author is definitely
ranked among the prophets (cf. 22:9). As were some
great prophets of the Old Testament (Is. 6:1-13;
Ezek. 1:1; 5:25) he is chosen in a grandiose vision
(1:9-19); he calls his revelation a prophecy (1:3) and
he values the prophetic office so highly that he sees
its testimony as working continually in the Church
until the end of time (11:1-14; cf. 19:10).

As a **Christian** prophecy Revelation knows that
Christ has given fulfillment to the revelations of the
Old Testament. Hence the abundant usage of Old
Testament writings, especially of Daniel (Christ as
the Son of Man: 1:12-16=Dan. 7:13), Ezek. (the

throne vision of God, 4:1-11 to be compared with Ezek. 1:5-21, 26-28), Exodus (8:7-12; 9:1-10; 16:3-7, 10-11, 21, to be compared with the plagues of Egypt in Ex. 7:14; 10:21; Rev. 15:3 to be compared with the passage through the Red Sea in Ex. 15:1-19).

The prophet John begins with the conviction that with Christ the end time has already come. Christ is the Lord. The kingdom of God and of Christ is already here on earth, an existent reality which is the Church. This faithful conviction must be more emphatically asserted in view of the tremendous persecutions and suffering to which the faithful are exposed by the earthly powers, representatives of the kingdom of satan.

The apocalyptic is allowed a glance at the development and the course of the events of the end time, which are already in a certain sense realized in the history of his own days in the immense struggle and the persecutions which the satanic powers carry on against the kingdom of God on earth. But his view also reaches the crowning of all those events in the parousia of the Son of Man and in the definitive dominion of God. A summarization of the whole of Revelation is strikingly expressed in 17:14: ". . . they will make war on the Lamb, and the Lamb will conquer them, for he is Lord of lords and King of kings, and those with him are called and chosen and faithful."

Thus Revelation is above all a book of hope and consolation, which, in view of the imminent return of Christ, prophetically admonishes the faithful to martyrdom, to believing testimony on behalf of Christ. It is a prophetic admonition to those whose devotion to God is threatened by the worldly spirit; it calls them back to their prior love (6:9; 11:7; 2:1; 3:22).

Revelation of God by word and deed in gospel and letters. Unlike Revelation which so explicitly professes to be "revelation," it may strike us that this same word is lacking in the other writings of John. Nevertheless his gospel and letters (especially the longer first letter) are dominated more by the notion of revelation than is the Apocalypse. Although the noun (revelation) does not occur, the verbs which indicate the various aspects of revelational actions are more numerous and play a central role (revealing, testifying, teaching, speaking). Even the theological terms he uses invoke revelational notions: life, light, truth, word, glory, work, sign.

His view of divine manifestation in the gospel and letters begins with a deep conviction about God's complete invisibility and hiddenness, seldom presented in this way in the Old Testament. The prologue, as a kind of overture gives the main theme of the gospel and with the signficant words: "No one has ever seen God" (1:18).[21] In these words, seemingly cold statements, the deepest desire of all religious mankind and especially of Judaism really vibrates: the hope of seeing God himself (Ex. 33:18-23; Ps. 17:15; 42:3; 63:2-3)!

Here John begins his gladdening message: God has not remained the great Hidden One, he has emerged from his secrecy: "The only God, who is toward the bosom of the Father, he has made him known" (1:18).[22] Though these words have a general meaning, we will first take them in the obvious sense of informing by means of **words**. These media of revelation, making salvation history known throughout the Old Testament were important means in the encounter between God and man; they also play the chief role in the revelation brought by Jesus (14:10-12; cf. 8:12-14; 10:35-38), so much so that the term, personified, is applied to Christ (the "Word").

The content of the words Jesus speaks to us is compactly summarized in the last verse of the prologue: "the only God, who is toward the bosom of the Father."

As God himself is one and manifold, so also his message is simple and complex. In the first place, Christ makes the Father known to us. This is the beginning and the end of his preaching, just as he himself and by himself finds rest only in his being with the Father (1:1, 18). He can summarize his entire earthly life work in this one sentence directed to the Father: "I have manifested thy name to the men whom thou gavest me" (17:6, 26). And the same revelation remains the summary of his preaching in the future: "The hour is coming when I shall no longer speak to you in figures but tell you plainly of the Father" (16:25; 17:26).

Only Jesus can make the Father known because
he himself is the Son. Thus the revelation of the
Father is at the same time the revelation of the Son:
"The Father loves the Son, and has given all things
into his hand. He who believes in the Son has eternal life; he who does not obey the Son shall not see
life, but the wrath of God rests upon him" (3:35-36).[23]
As both are one (10:30; 17:11, 21-23; 14:20), it is
impossible to separate the preaching of the Father
from the revelation of the Son and vice versa: "They
said to him therefore: Where is your Father? Jesus
answered: You know neither me nor my father; if
you knew me you would know my Father also"
(8:19).[24]

We can even say that only in Christ do we find
the revelation of the Father: "No one comes to the
Father, but by me" (14:6; cf. 1 Jn. 2:22-23). Outside
him, we seek knowledge of the Father in vain. Others
to be sure could testify in favor of Christ (5:33, 46).
But they were unable to speak about God from the
experience of one who has seen God. The reason
for this lies in the strict separation between heaven
and earth; this is distinctive of John's theology. It
considers God as absolutely exalted above the world.
He sends messengers, to be sure, but these are "men,
sent by God" (1:6). The essential distance which still
separates them from God implies that their testimony
can rightly be called the language of the earth,
because they — just as all the others — are from the
earth and belong to the earth (3:31). Only one may
really speak about God as revealing him in truth:

"Truly, truly, I say to you: we speak of what we know, and bear witness to what we have seen . . . No one has ascended into heaven but he who descended from heaven, the Son of Man" (3:11, 13; cf. 6:46).

This last sentence is also an example of the continuity between the revelation brought by Jesus Christ and the revelation of the Old Covenant. Jesus here presents himself as the fulfillment of the prophecy about the Son of Man, the mysterious figure in Daniel (Dan. 7:13-14) and in similar writings of later Judaism. He is the embodiment of the transcendent messianic ideal of the apocalyptics and who, as such, already pre-exists with God. But at the same time he joins with it the view of the personified **Wisdom** of sapiential literature, who acted as the pre-existing confidant of God, knowing his secrets and deputed by him to go down to the world and there preach the divine wisdom (Wis. 9:16-18; Bar. 3:29, 37-38; Prov. 30:3-4). Thus Jesus unites the central contents of apocalyptic belief with wisdom in order to express, as Son of Man and personified Wisdom, his unique function in revelation.

He also treats the typical topics of both those milieus, when he speaks about the so very important notion of truth and applies it to himself (cf. Dan. 9:13; 10:21; Wis. 3:9; 6:22). As a ruler whose kingdom is not of this world he has come into the world in order to preach the heavenly secrets as an eye-witness, in an inviting way and at the price of his life (Jn. 18:37). He himself is the truth, that is, he

himself as the incarnated word and the Son of God
who in his very being is the revelation of the Father
and thus the way to the Father (14:6).

The Son of God reveals the Father and himself
not only by his spoken word but by his works, which
he calls **signs,** because they point to a higher reality.

The signs have, on the lowest level, an apologetic
value, because they reveal Jesus as the one sent by
God to act authoritatively in his name (2:3; 3:2).

But on a higher level, they have, literally, a
theological significance; they manifest God himself
in Jesus. Like the most important words of Christ,
so also his signs can be interpreted as a revelation
of the Father: "Philip said to him: Lord, show us
the Father, and we shall be satisfied. Jesus said to
him: Have I been with you so long, and yet you do
not know me, Philip? . . . The words that I say
to you I do not speak on my own authority;
but the Father who dwells in me does his works.
Believe me that I am in the Father and the Father
in me; or else believe me for the sake of the works
themselves" (14:8-11). But the same signs can equiv-
alently be directly referred to the Son as revealing
his divine glory: "Jesus . . . manifested his glory; and
his disciples believed in him" (2:11).[25]

Revelation as redemption. Consequent to their
strictly theological significance, these signs also have
a revelational value which is redemptive or soteriological. In the sermon commenting on the miracle of
the loaves Christ's function as the bread of life is

coupled with his divine origin: "My Father gives to
you the true bread from heaven. For the bread of
God is that which comes down from heaven, and
gives life to the world" (6:32-33; cf. 6:41-42). The
signs, continued in the sacraments (cf. chapters 6 and
9), really show that the eschatological salvation of
the messianic time has come (20:31). As a medium
of revelation where God's redemption is shown in
deeds, the signs could be compared with the synoptic
miracles. But unlike these, which chiefly are directed
to the kingdom of God, in this fourth gospel they
are explicitly connected with the person of Christ;
they reveal him as the divine Redeemer.

Christ often expresses this redeeming aspect of
his person on the occasion of a miraculous sign by
using the formula, "I am." If there is no further
determination, this decidedly has a theological meaning. The mysterious "I am" Jesus uses in Jn. 8:24
to express the essence of saving faith (cf. 8:28),
achieves its final form excluding all doubt: "Truly,
truly, I say to you, before Abraham was, I am"
(8:58). Jesus here appropriates the formula of self-
representation by which Yahweh, from his hiddenness, came to Moses and the Jewish people and revealed himself to Israel (Ex. 3:14; cf. Ex. 20:2; Is.
41:4; 46:4).

There is opposition between the variable "becoming" and the permanent "being" (before Abraham
was, I 'am); this can only be fully understood from a
Greek world view. But this self-represenation formula
of John shows development — in accord with the

Old Testament example — toward God's active being and his redeeming action. As Christ can apply the "I am" formula to himself, he also can develop it further: "I am the bread of life" (6:35, 38), "I am the light of the world" (8:12), "I am the good shepherd" (10:11, 14). These soteriological formulas in their turn lead up to the all-encompassing, "I am the resurrection and the life" (11:25); here we find succinct expression of the fact that revelation is directed to salvation. Revealed truth leads those who faithfully accept the person of the Redeemer to life: "I am the light of the world; he who follows me will not walk in darkness, but will have the light of life" (8:12).

We should note that life and salvation ultimately tend to love and union, to personal encounter. The life promised to man is resurrection from bodily and spiritual death (11:23-26), but it is much more than this. It does not allow man to complacently rest in himself; it insists that he go beyond himself and enter into loving knowledge and communion with the Father and the Son: "This is eternal life, that they know thee, the only true God, and Jesus Christ whom thou hast sent" (17:3; cf. 6:57).

The Incarnation as the fundamental revealing deed. Summarizing, we might express the entire revelatory activity of the John's Christ by the revealing deed which is the basis of his prologue, (1:14) and of the introduction to his first letter (1 Jn. 1:2): the incarnation of the Word.

The literary structure of the prologue, in keeping with a semitic stylistic process, makes the end correspond with the beginning (the so-called **inclusio**); this shows that the Word or Logos is seen as the revealing Word the Father speaks in his Son; in him, as in an image, he expresses himself completely; the living Word turned toward the bosom of the Father and could make the Father known (1:18). This is confirmed by the words of the first verse: the Word was with God (1:1). In his revealing function the Word may be seen as the definitive climax of the prophetic word which God in the course of history addressed, by way of self-revelation, to Israel.

The Logos possesses power greater than any other divine word. He is active in the creation and in history, he is the life of all being (1:3-4). He is the Word of creation and the Word of life (Jn. 1:1-2). Here we have the basis of the vivifying activity which he, having been incarnated, shall continue in his works: "My Father is working still, and I am working" (5:17).

This however does not exhaust the riches of the Logos-theology. What John says in the prologue about the intimacy of the Word with the Father and about his activity in creation and salvation history clearly shows that he has included the concept of Logos as personified wisdom (as regards intimacy of the Word with the Father: Jn. 1:1, 2, 18; and his presence at the creation: Jn. 1:3-4; cf. Prov. 8:22-31; Sir. 24:3-4; Wis. 7:21; 8:6; 9:9; as to the descent into

the world: Jn. 1:9-14; cf. Sir. 24:6-11; Wis. 9:9; 11:17).
Moreover the prologue seems to indicate some dis-
agreement with rabbinic opinions (cf. Sir. 24:23)
which identified the personified wisdom with the law,
the center of Judaism in those days. When John
writes: "The law was given through Moses, grace
and truth came through Jesus Christ" (1:17) he
probably wants to teach us that the Word, gifted
with all the endowment of wisdom, has taken the
place of the law.

About this Word the prologue pronounces as its
most overwhelming testimony, "The Word became
flesh and dwelt among us" (1:14a). Incarnation really
is a terminus and a synthesis of all former revealing
deeds and self-revelations of God. God here has
entered into world history in the most personal way.
He who is has become. By being what he is —
incarnated Word and Son — Christ is the revelation
of God. This divine revealing deed alone made
possible every other revelation by word and deed
of John's Christ. This entry of God into mankind,
into the flesh — a revelation of his love for men
(1 Jn. 4:9) — is the foundation for identification of
God's revelation with history, of word and sacrament,
of tradition and Church. The incarnation — the
fundamental revealing deed — rather than the resurrection is the central theme of John's theology of
revelation (although resurrection plays an important
role in making the disciples conscious of Christ's
divinity and messianic dignity: cf. 14:18-20; 20:24-29;
2:22; 12:6). For John, in fine, incarnation of the

Word is revelation, manifestation: "The life was made manifest, and we saw it, and testify to it, and proclaim to you the eternal life which was with the Father and was made manifest to us" (1 Jn. 1:2; cf. 3:5, 8).

Seeing and believing. The incarnated Word has broken through the invisibility of God. No one has ever seen God, but in Christ he has appeared to us. This is why John's theology gives major prominence to "seeing" as man's response to revelation (1:14, 50, 51; 4:45; 6:2; 11:40; 13:24; 19:35; 1 Jn. 1:1-3; 4:14). The stress given this term may be explained, it is true, by the general New Testament conviction that with Christ the end time has arrived. According to the Biblical view, the eschatological time is distinguished by the seeing of God's glory (cf. Is. 40:5; 60:1-3, 19-20). But this emphasis should be ascribed rather to the specifically personal view of the evangelist that God himself has become visible for the first time in Christ: "He who has seen me has seen the Father" (14:9; 1:14). In giving prominence to seeing, John's view of revelation is clearly distinguished from the Old Testament stance in which revelation, mainly concentrated in the word (of the law or the prophet), is received first of all by hearing.

A special climactic text describes the incarnated Word not only as visible, but even tangible: "That which was from the beginning, which we have heard, which we have seen with our eyes, which we have looked upon and touched with our hands, concerning the word of life" (1 Jn. 1:1). But this too explains the nature of **seeing** more fully: God's visi-

bility in Christ is an experience gradually developing
itself by intimate contact with the incarnate Word;
in this process faith has its continuing role. For
the privileged witnesses, who later must spread the
message of God's appearance in Christ, faith is not
replaced by bodily seeing, but is implied in it.
Bodily seeing must be impregnated by a spiritual
seeing: "Have I been with you so long, and yet you
do not know me, Philip? He who has seen me has
seen the Father . . . Believe me that I am in the
Father and the Father in me; or else believe me for
the sake of the works themselves" (14:9-11).

Thus Christ's words, "Blessed are those who have
not seen and yet believe" (20:29) — though addressed
immediately to the hearers of the testifying word —
also applies to the circle of eye-witnesses. The word
of the revealing Christ here too retains its importance
as a necessary means of revelation, continually
insisting on man's belief. Earthly existence, although
it has acquired an eschatological dimension by the
incarnation, continues to be subject to faith; this is
the human response to revelation, and life or death
depend on it (1:12; 3:15-18, 36; 5:24; 6:40, 47; 8:24;
11:25-26; 12:46; 20:31; 1 Jn. 3:23-24; 4:15-16; 5:1-13).

The leap which must be taken in order to comply
with the demands of the revealing word and the
offense connected with the idea of the Word's "becoming flesh" is in part determined by man's decision. But faith is also a gift from the Father. Christ
who reveals the Father (and himself) by the incarnation, his visible actions, his words and in an

exceptional way by flashes of his divine glory, must be revealed by the Father on another level if man is to acknowledge him really as the Son of Man who came down from heaven. In a text consociated with Jeremiah's promise of a general eschatological revelation (Jer. 31:33-34; Is. 54:13). John's Christ teaches us: "No one can come to me unless the Father who sent me draws him . . . It is written in the prophets: And they shall all be taught by God. Every one who has heard and learned from the Father comes to me" (6:44-45). Thus we have here a wonderful continuity in which the Father leads believing man to the Son, and through the Son to himself.

Revelation of the Spirit and tradition. But the circle of revelation is not yet closed. After the ascension of Christ, his return to the Father, a third Person enters into the communion of the divine persons who reveal and are being revealed: the Spirit of truth.

That he is a person is immediately expressed in the first words in which Christ presents him in his farewell speech: "And I will pray the Father, and he will give you another Counselor, to be with you for ever, even the Spirit of truth . . ." (14:16-17); he is another helper, as Jesus himself had hitherto been (cf. 1 Jn. 2:1). Further assertions, referring to his proceeding from the Father (15:26) and his perfect knowledge of the Son (14:25; 16:12-16) suggest his divine nature. His revealing assistance is explicitly promised to the apostles; the Holy Spirit himself will instruct them and communicate the truth to them:

"The Counselor, the Holy Spirit, whom the Father will
send in my name, he will teach you all things, and
bring to your remembrance all that I have said to
you" (14:26). This instruction concerns the person of
Christ and his doctrine. In this way it reawakens the
memories of all the earthly Christ said and did; but
as we know, in Biblical language such remembrance
does not consist only in a material recall of past
words and deeds, but also in actualizing them and
in revealing their deeper and more spiritual sense.
The activity of the Spirit obviously comprises another
element of additional value: he guides the disciples
to **all** truth; he reveals the many things which Jesus
during his mortal life still had to say but could
not say, because they were not able to bear them.
This revelation too is directed to the mystery of
Christ, who is truth itself: "I have yet many things
to say to you, but you cannot bear them now. When
the Spirit of truth comes, he will guide you into all
the truth; for he will not speak on his own authority,
but whatever he hears he will speak, and he will
declare you the things that are to come. He will
glorify me, for he will take what is mine and declare it to you. All that the Father has is mine;
therefore I said that he will take what is mine and
declare it to you" (16:12-15).

This revelatory function of the Spirit remains inti-
mately united with the office of the apostles, who
must testify about Christ. It is the Spirit who speaks
in and through the apostles' testimony: "But when
the Counselor comes, whom I shall send to you

from the Father, even the Spirit of truth, who proceeds from the Father, he will bear witness to me; and you also are witnesses, because you have been with me from the beginning" (15:26-27).

These teachings of John, written at the end of the apostolic time, legitimize the unfolding and the evolution of the mystery of Christ; this was expressed after Jesus' death in oral tradition and greatly affected John's own testimony in his (written) gospel. The Spirit of truth, who is the Spirit of Christ himself, has himself led the apostles into these deeper insights about Christ. The promise, quoted in Jn. 14:16-17, that the assistance of the Spirit is to be given to the disciples "for ever" — that is for an everlasting duration — evidently intends to determine the structure of the Church and assure her position after the death of the apostles in the persons of their successors. At first sight, there seems to be an obvious tension and even a seeming contradiction between these texts, if we want to harmonize them. The one says that the Spirit of truth will remain with the disciples (14:16-17); this must also include those who shall take their place. In the other text however the testimony of the Spirit of truth about Christ is bound to the preaching of the apostles who give their testimony because of their physical presence with him from the beginning of his ministry (15:26-37). This last detail indeed hints at a special position of the witnesses by eye and ear, which is no longer true for their successors. We suggest that a solution can be found in this way: this special intimacy with the Spirit of truth on the part of the eye-witnesses indicates that their testimony has a normative value for all their successors; but these nevertheless are also directly gifted with the assistance of the Spirit of truth.

Just how the oral testimony of the apostles is related to Scripture is not apodictically answered in John's gospel. The assertion, "These (signs) are written that you may believe that Jesus is the Christ, the Son of God, and that believing you may have life in his name" does give the impression that his own testimony about Christ was substantially incorporated into his gospel. Does the immediately preceding verse point to the deposit which the various testimonies concerning Christ, found by other eye-witnesses in other New Testament writings (Now Jesus did many other signs in the presence of the disciples, which are not written in this book")? Or must this saying be understood more generally as pointing to an oral tradition **not wrtiten down at all?** This latter explication might perhaps find considerable support in the verses at the **end** of the gospel, the last of which, hyperbolical in form, perhaps wishes to express a theological truth: "This is the disciple who is bearing witness to these things, and who has written these things: and we know that his testimony is exact. But there are also many other things which Jesus did; were every one of them to be written, I suppose that the world itself could not contain the books that would be written" (21: 24-25).

In any case, the Spirit of truth continually points to the preaching of eye-witnesses, in leading the Church to knowledge of the entire mystery of Christ. This knowledge is also love. It is the task of the Holy Spirit to awaken in the bride — the Church — the desire for the return of Christ: "The Spirit and the Bride say: Come . . . Amen. Come, Lord Jesus" (Rev. 21:17, 20). Only at the appearance of Christ in the parousia will the final goal of God's manifestation, begun with the incarnation of the Word be reached. Then the prayer of Christ to the Father will be fulfilled: "Father, I desire that they also, whom thou hast given me, may be with me where I am, to behold my glory which thou hast given me in thy love for me before the foundation of the world" (Jn. 17:24).

God's glory, to be fully reevaled only then, already now sheds its radiance on the life of every Christian and fills it with its radiance in the life of every Christian and fills it with holiness, in the hope of the great revelation (1 Jn. 3:2-3):

>"We know that when he appears
>we shall be like him,
>for we shall see him as he is."

REFERENCES

1. Cf. Ex. 14:17, 18; 15:6, 11-13.

2. Cf. also, with some variant readings, Ezek. 7:26; Mich. 3:11.

3. Cf. Judg. 20:18, 23, 27; 1 Sam. 14:18, 37; 22:10.

4. Even the New Testament still knows a "prophetic" gift of the high priest: cf. Jn. 11:51-52!

5. Cf. Lam. 3:55-57; Ps. 20:1-6/7; 41:11/12.

6. Cf. Mt. 2:37=Mk. 12:30=Lk. 10:27.

7. Cf. Ps. 89:27-40; 132:11-12.

8. Cf. 1 Kings 17:1; 18:17; Is. 9:7; 55:10-11.

9. We here have an example in Hos. 1:4-5 how a new prophecy removes a former prophetic word (2 Kings 9:1-12).

10. The whole passage is to be read, starting from verse 20; cf. also Dan. 2:30; 5:11, 14; 12:3, and 1:4; 2:18.

11. Cf. 1 Sam. 10:12; 1 Kings 20:11.

12. Cf. the resemblance of Prov. 25:6 and Lk. 14:8-11, the texts from Prov. 3:11-12 in Heb. 12:5-6, and those of Prov. 25:21-22 in Rom. 12:20.

13. Cf. Eccles. 3:10-11; 8:17; 11:5.

14. Cf. Prov. 1:8; 4:1; 31:1; Sir. 3:1.

15. To be conferred with the solution of the problem of retribution — in the line of the specifically Hebrew setting off of the bodiliness of man — in Dan. 12:1-3 and 2 Macc. 7:9, 11, 14, 23, 29; 12:41-46; 14:46.

16. Cf. Ps. 106:9-12; Is. 7:9; 28:16.

17. Cf. Ps. 30:10; 88:11-13; 115:17.

18. Cf. Ps. 8:19a; 104; Wis. 13; Acts 14:17; 17:16-31.

19. Cf. Col. 2:2-3; 4:3.

20. Cf. also Eph. 3:5; 1 Cor. 2:9-13.

21. Cf. Jn. 6:46; 1 Jn. 4:20.

22. The translation: "Who is turned toward the bosom of the Father" seems to us the best in order to render the dynamic force of the Greek preposition *eis* used here.

23 Cf. Jn. 5:19-26; 10:36; 11:4, 27; 14:13.

24. Cf. Jn. 10:38; 14:7, 10, 11; 17:21.

25. Cf. Jn. 5:19-23, 36; 20:31.